Contents

Chapter		Page
1	The Birth of the King	7
2	The Royal Child	10
3	The King's Herald	14
4	The Testing of the King	19
5	The Laws of the Kingdom	25
6	The Laws of the Kingdom (cont'd)	35
7	The Laws of the Kingdom (cont'd)	40
8	Miracles of the King	45
9	Miracles of the King (cont'd)	58
10	Twelve Apostles Sent Out	65
11	Opposition to the King	72
12	The King Greater than All	79
13	The Kingdom in Parables	85
14	The Power of the King	93
15	The King's Teaching and Miracles	96
16	The Great Confession	100
17	The Glory of the King	106
18	Teaching about the Church	110
19	Teaching about the Family and Young People	114
20	The Servants of the King	117
21	The King Enters the Holy City	121
22	The King and Leaders of Israel	126
23	The King and Leaders of Israel (cont'd)	131
24	The King Foretells Future Events	136
25	The King Foretells Future Events (cont'd)	140
26	The King Betrayed and Condemned	144
27	The King Crucified	154
28	The Risen King	165

Introduction

The book of Matthew stands at the gateway from the Old Testament into the New Testament. In the Old Testament we find many prophecies foretelling the coming of a promised Deliverer and King. These prophecies are like identification pictures or photographs which describe what the coming King would be like, what He would do and what would happen to Him.

The Spirit of God directed Matthew to present the Lord Jesus Christ as the King to the nation of Israel. So Matthew makes many references to Israel's Bible, the Old Testament writings. Matthew looked back into those Old Testament books and found many of these "identity pictures." As he writes the story he includes many of these pictures so that Israel (and all of us) might recognize this great King and bow down to worship and obey Him.

Of course the other New Testament writers also quote from the Old Testament, but Matthew does so much more than the others. Apart from the genealogies there are over 250 direct and indirect references to the Old Testament in his book. He quotes from every book in the Old Testament except five (Ecclesiastes, Song of Solomon, Obadiah, Nahum and Habakkuk). In a sense Matthew is like a gatekeeper who carefully identifies the One who is the promised Deliverer-King. (See John 10.1-3). He proves over and over that Jesus Christ is the real King by comparing Him with those pictures in the Old Testament. As we go through Matthew's book together you may want to notice each picture and write down the references in your Bible.

In chapters 1-2 we will read about the genealogy and birth of this great King.

In chapter 3 we see the King's herald and fore-runner.

In chapters 4-18 we find the King's public life of service, mostly in Galilee.

In chapters 19-20 the King goes from Galilee to Jerusalem, the City of the great King.

In chapters 21-27 He is in Jerusalem as the rejected King, condemned and put to death.

In chapter 28 He rises from the dead and appears to His followers.

The reader may find it helpful to mark the King's journeys on a map. See if your Bible has a good map in the back. As you read through Matthew find each place He visited and draw lines from place to place. You may want to draw a larger map of your own to keep the lines separate as He went back and forth. You will notice that most of the time was spent in Galilee, until chapter 21. We will see why later on.

Chapter 1
The Birth of the King

A king must have royal ancestors to have right to the throne. There must be a record of his family lineage. So Matthew introduces Jesus Christ as a descendant of King David and of Abraham. Abraham was the father of the Jewish people. He was the first one to receive a direct promise from God that the coming Deliverer would be from his family, Genesis 22.18. King David, Israel's greatest king, was the last one to receive such a promise, 1 Chronicles 17.11-14.

Jesus is the New Testament name for the combination of two Old Testament names meaning Jehovah the Savior, or, The Salvation of the Lord.

The name Christ in the New Testament and Messiah in the Old Testament both mean the Anointed One. In Old Testament times the prophets, priests and kings in Israel were anointed with oil. That is, oil was poured on them as a sign of special office. So this name tells us that Jesus is God's anointed and appointed King and Savior. We are going to see how Matthew presents Him in this special way.

2-17 In verses 2-17 the ancestors of Jesus Christ are traced from Abraham through David to Joseph and Mary the mother of Jesus. This is divided into three parts of Israel's history and each part includes 14 persons. This was probably done as an easy way to remember the genealogy:

1. From Abraham to King David, vs. 1-6
2. From Solomon to Israel's Exile, to King Jehoikim (as we suggest v. 11 should read) vs. 7-11.
3. From Exile, (King Jeconiah) to Jesus Christ, vs. 12-16.

If you trace the Old Testament history of the kings you will find three that were omitted here (Ahaziah, Joash and Amaziah). This probably was because of their connection with the wicked king Ahab and Jezebel. But the interesting thing to note here is that four women are listed in this genealogy. Usually this was not done by Jewish recorders, but the Holy Spirit directed Matthew to mention them here: Tamar, v. 3; Rahab, v. 5; Ruth, v. 5; Bathsheba, wife of Uriah, v. 6. All of them tell us about the grace of God. Each is linked with sin: Tamar reminds us of the sin of Judah, Genesis 38; Rahab was a prostitute, Joshua 6; Ruth suffered because of Naomi's and Elimelech's disobedience, Ruth 1; and Bathsheba was linked with king David's sin in 2 Samuel 11. But each woman was listed with the ancestors of our

Lord Jesus by the great grace of God. "Where sin abounded God's grace has abounded much more," Romans 5.20. It is the same wonderful grace of God that places us, as unworthy sinners, in HIS family when we receive Jesus Christ as our Savior, by faith. Are you in HIS family?

Some readers may wonder why Matthew's genealogy is different from Luke's. Very briefly we would mention that Matthew presents Jesus as King, so he traces His ancestors through king David via Solomon for the line of royal title down to Joseph. Luke traces Mary's ancestors through king David's son Nathan, Luke 3.31. Luke goes right back to Adam because he presents Jesus as the Son of Man. Matthew presents Jesus as Israel's king back through David to Abraham.

So in this way Matthew introduces the King to Israel and to the world. He gives us proof that Jesus is great David's greater Son with every right to the throne of Israel.

The Royal Birth, 1.18-25

Joseph, the carpenter of Nazareth, was engaged to be married to Mary. This engagement was as binding as marriage itself regarding purity and loyalty. Joseph was a man who did what was right, and Mary was a virgin. So it must have been a shock to him to learn that Mary was pregnant before they were actually living together. What should he do? The Jewish law was clear that if he exposed her publicly as a wicked, unfaithful girl, she should be put to death, Deuteronomy 22.22-24. But he could privately give her a paper of divorce and break the engagement-marriage legally, Deuteronomy 24.1. No doubt his heart was heavy as he thought about this during the night.

But an angel appeared to him in a dream and explained what had happened. Mary had conceived by the Holy Spirit of God. The new baby was to be more than just a man; He was the Son of God, Luke 1.35. Joseph was also told what name to give the baby: **JESUS**. And the reason for that name: *He will save His people from their sins.*

How happy Joseph must have felt! The long-promised Savior was coming, and to live in **his** home! The Old Testament promise was being fulfilled after all those centuries!

Now we find the first "identity picture" from the Old Testament. Matthew quotes from Isaiah 7. Find the verse where Isaiah foretold that a virgin, an unmarried young woman, would give birth to a son and name him Immanuel (which means: God with us). Also find two verses in Isaiah 8 which tell about Immanuel, God with us.

So now Joseph understood God's wonderful Secret, 1 Timothy 3.16. It was necessary that Jesus be born of the virgin. If Joseph were the blood-father of Jesus, He would have been born a sinner just like all of us. Then He could never be our Savior, He would have to die for His own sins. But God's plans were perfect. Joseph was told to take Mary home as his wife. He was to accept the **legal** responsibility for the child. And this is what Joseph did, v. 24. When the baby was born Joseph, His legal guardian, gave Him that precious name — JESUS.

Jesus, oh how sweet the Name;
Jesus, let all earth proclaim
His worthy praise forever!

And the other name of the King is Immanuel, God with us. Who can understand the wonder of it all? The great Creator of the universe came down to live among mankind, John 1.3,14. He came to seek and save lost sinners, Luke 19.10. He came to save us from our sins. Praise His Name!

Chapter 2

The Royal Child

1 Matthew now tells us that Christ was born in Bethlehem in Judea, which was about 5 miles (7 kilometers) south of Jerusalem. It was during the reign of King Herod the Great. Herod had been appointed king of Judea by the Emperor of Rome. But to most Jews he was a foreigner who had no claim to the throne. Actually he was an Edomite, that is a descendant of Esau who sold his birthright, Genesis 25.29-34. The real throne of David was empty. The nation of Israel should have been expecting their true King at any time. But they were not.

2 But some other people were looking for Him. Somewhere to the east of Judea there were some men called Magi or wise men. They were men who studied the stars. They may have been high-ranking officials in their country. (Compare Jeremiah 39.3,13 where this title occurs in some old Bibles). We do not know for sure where their home was, but they must have been very important men, and wealthy. Best of all they were looking for a Child who had been born King of the Jews.

So they came to Jerusalem, the capital city, where they would expect to find Him. They asked, "Where is He that is born King of the Jews?" They had seen His star back home in the east country and they came to worship Him.

This star may have been a special star or comet sent by God at just the right time to signal the birth of the great King. (God is perfectly able to do such a miracle!) God gave this "sign" in order to cause those Wise Men to leave home in search for the new King. They probably traveled at least four months or longer to Jerusalem, see Ezra 7.9.

Why did they call the star "**His** star"? They were not Jews but they may have heard about the verse in Numbers 24.17 which had foretold a Star arising out of Jacob (Israel).

3 Verse 3 tells us that these visitors caused people in Jerusalem to be greatly upset, especially Herod. He knew about the Jewish belief that a Messiah was promised. He did not like the idea of some other king taking over his territory.

4 So he called together the religious rulers of the people, the chief priests and scribes (teachers of the law). These men would surely be able to tell where the promised King was to be born. Yes, they could and did so right away. And here is another "identity picture" from the Old Testament. It is found in Micah 5.2. (Look it up and mark it in your Bible).

5,6 "In Bethlehem" was the answer. Compare Matthew 2.1. Bethlehem means "the house of bread." It is where the Bread from Heaven, our Lord Jesus, came down to bring life and satisfaction to hungry, needy men and women. See John 6.33-51.

7,8 Herod then called the Wise Men for a secret, private meeting. He asked them exactly when they had seen the star. Then he told them to go to Bethlehem, search carefully for that child and report back to him so he could also worship Him. Of course, he did not really intend to worship Him; he hated Him and wanted to kill Him.

So the new King had enemies already. Herod's hatred was more than mere human hatred. Behind Herod moved "enemy number one," Satan, the devil himself, the old serpent, the great dragon. We read about him in Revelation 12.1-9. There it is explained how Satan tried to destroy the new King as soon as He came to earth. Back in the Old Testament he had tried various ways to destroy the royal line and prevent Christ's coming to earth.

And during Christ's life on earth Satan attempted to kill Him before His time, for example, see Luke 4.28-30. Do you know of any other such times? (* See Footnote)

9 Of course the Wise Men knew nothing about Herod's plans. They hurried on their way and were overjoyed to see "the star" again, low over Bethlehem, right by the house where the Child was. Their long search was ended.

10,11 What a thrill filled their hearts as they saw the Child! What was their response?
They bowed down before Him.
They offered gifts to Him.
He was only a Child—but they recognized Him: a King.
He was only a few months old—yet they knew He was
                      from Eternity (see Micah 5.2 again).
He was a "human" baby—but they worshiped Him as God.

---

*Footnote: The serious Bible student would be interested in looking at the following references which we have no space to deal with here: Genesis 3.15; 4.1-8,25; 6.1,2; 16.1-4; Exodus chaps. 1-14. Compare Genesis 49.10 with 1 Samuel 23.14; 2 Samuel 7.12,13; 1 Kings 1.17; 2 Kings 11.1-3; 12.1.

How could they recognize GOD in this little child? We can be sure the Holy Spirit had revealed it to them by that verse in Micah. The entrance of God's Word gives light, Psalm 119.130. Their eyes were opened to behold the King Himself in that little form. So they at once opened their treasures and presented their offerings to Him. This is the same word as is used of offerings to God in Hebrews 5.1; 8.3,4; 9.9, and many other times. This Child was God Himself in human form. What a wonderful truth! No wonder they bowed and worshiped Him. Have you done so?

Their gifts were: **Gold**—this spoke of Christ's Deity, Glory
Incense—fragrance, beauty of His Holiness
Myrrh—used in burying people; spoke of Death.

How touching! The Divine One, the Holy One, born a King, was also born to die—for you and me!

12 What a contrast between Herod, the hateful murderer, and these Wise Men, loving and worshiping! Herod planned to kill the innocent Child, but God had other plans. We now note four dreams in which the Angel of the Lord appeared—first to the Wise Men. They were warned not to return to Herod, so they obeyed and went home by another road.

13 Then in verse 13 Joseph is warned in a dream to leave Bethlehem at once and take the Child and His mother to Egypt for safety.

14,15 Joseph obeyed at once. Another "identity picture" is applied here—Hosea 11.1, *Out of Egypt I called my Son*. Out of Bethlehem came the promised Ruler. Out of Egypt came the Son of God. This is another witness to the Deity of our Lord Jesus Christ. He was only a child at this time but He was the Son of God all the time.

16-18 Herod became very angry when he found out that the Wise Men had tricked him. But it was really God who had spoiled Herod's plans. God was mocking him, Psalm 2.1-4. No hands could be laid on God's Son until His hour would come, John 7.30. But wicked Herod ordered that all boys in Bethlehem area, under two years old, be killed. In this way he thought he could kill this new King.

It is sad to read how the brokenhearted mothers wailed and wept for their lost children. But even this was another "identity picture" referring to the coming of the King. It is found in Jeremiah 31.15. Matthew relates this to the present grief of these mothers. The tomb of Rachel was just about a mile (2 kilometers) north of Bethlehem. Matthew says this weeping was like the weeping of Rachel, the mother of Israel, weeping on behalf of her children as she looked over Bethlehem that sad day.

Matthew 2.12-23

19 Verse 19 tells us that Herod died. God punished him for his great crime. The destroyer was destroyed himself. This reminds us that God is still on the Throne of the Universe. He notices every wrong, hears every cry, and counts every tear. He is going to punish every sinner sooner or later. Herod died. The wages of sin is death, Romans 6.23.

20-22 Once again the Lord spoke to Joseph in a second dream, "Go back home to Israel, it's safe now." So Joseph returned with the Child and His mother. Then in a third dream He told him to go to the province of Galilee instead of Judea. So they settled in a little town called Nazareth. Here another "identity picture" is linked with Messiah's experiences:

23 The prophet's word was fulfilled, He will be called a Nazarene.

Only in this case no specific Old Testament reference can be found which uses just those words.

Nazareth was a place of bad reputation and was held in contempt by many, see John 1.46. For Jesus to be from Nazareth would be a rather shameful thing. This might remind us of verses like Isaiah 53.1-3. The Lord on earth was always humble. Some Bible teachers think Isaiah 11.1 is referred to, by the title Branch of the Lord. The Hebrew word there is *Netzer* meaning a twig or sprout in contrast to a mighty tree. (The word sounds like Nazarene.)

Our Lord was born in a humble manger, Luke 2.16, in a humble town, Micah 5.2; and moved to despised, humble childhood in Nazareth. But in spite of all that we must notice how very **important** this Child is in this chapter: HE was born a King, v. 2; HIS star, v.2; Ruler and Shepherd, v.6; search for THE child, worship HIM, v.8; the place where the Child was, v.9. Notice how HE is always mentioned before Mary: verses 11,13,14,20,21, They bowed down and worshiped HIM, v.11; offered gifts to HIM, v.11; searched for the Child, v.13; called My Son, v.15; the Child's life, v.20. Sixteen times HE is preeminent.

Chapter 3

The King's Herald

In ancient times the Eastern conquerors used to send heralds ahead of them to announce their coming. They told the people to prepare "the King's highway" for the royal carriages and armies. The greater the king the more splendid were his heralds. They would be dressed in beautiful, colorful clothes or uniforms. Loud trumpets would call the attention of everyone.

1 Matthew's account of the herald of our great King is very different.

John the Baptizer appears suddenly in the wild deserts of Judea along the southern part of the Jordan river. But there is no beating of drums neither are there trumpets and banners. Instead we see a very plain man in plain, poor clothing. And he begins his preaching in very plain language. But he speaks with authority.

Can this be the true herald of the great King? Where are all the attendant angels we would expect to see if he were really the forerunner of the King of kings? How can we know if he is genuine? Well, let's read what Matthew says about him.

2 John's first recorded word in REPENT! That is a sharp command.

It cuts like a sword into the heart. It says, Turn away from your sins, change direction. The basic thought behind it is this: Sorrow out of which comes a change.

The reason for this command is then given by John: The Kingdom of Heaven is near. So he has a message about a kingdom, but it is the kingdom of heaven. This term is found in Matthew about 30 times. In other places we read about the kingdom of God. In general these two names are referring to the same thing, but Matthew is writing specially for Jews. From the prophet Daniel (2.34-44; 7.23-27) we learn that the God of heaven would set up His kingdom on earth. We will be learning more about this as we go through Matthew.

What makes John's message so urgent is this: the Kingdom is near at hand. This should startle the people of Israel. They must have become very excited. But first the question must be answered — How can we know for sure that John the Baptizer is a true herald?

3 In verse 3 Matthew again brings out an "identity picture" for Israel to be able to recognize the herald of the great King. He refers to Isaiah 40.3. John is the man pictured there. He was going to call out in the desert as a voice for God, *Prepare the highway of the Lord — get* *ready for His coming!* That is just what John was doing. His work was to announce how the people could get ready.

The kingdom was not going to be at first a political, physical one. First it was to be a spiritual kingdom. That is, the King was not going to do away with the Roman empire and set Israel free politically just then. Instead He would deal first with the more important problem of sin and slavery to Satan. The kingdom was to be individual and internal, that is, in the heart, see Luke 17.21.

We suggest you turn to Isaiah 40 and read the whole chapter right now before going further in this book. Notice how beautifully the prophet describes what John's message would be and then goes on to describe the great King-Shepherd and Creator Himself, our Lord Jesus Christ. As you read about Him worship and praise Him.

4 The herald's clothing was very plain, woven of camel's hair. A leather belt was around his waist. This would all remind Israel of Elijah the prophet, 2 Kings 1.8; Zechariah 13.4. And his food was very plain, too—poor man's food, not expensive delicacies, rare meats and wines, only locusts or grasshoppers along with wild honey he found in the desert places. See Leviticus 11.22; Deuteronomy 32.13. In none of this would John be calling attention to himself.

Why was the great King's herald such a lowly, common kind of man? Because the King he represented was going to be lowly, humble, living and working among poor people. The common people would be listening to Him gladly, Mark 12.37. Why no soft clothing and costly palace feastings (chap. 11.8)? Because the King had left the Palace of heaven to come down to meet us in our deep need.

5,6 John's preaching was with power and deep feeling. Crowds came to hear him and kept coming from all around the countryside as well as from Jerusalem. Their consciences were reached and they confessed their sins and repented of them. As a witness to their change of heart they were baptized by John, v. 11. They went down into the waters of Jordan as he baptized them; that is, he put them down into the water and brought them out again. That is what the word baptize means. It was like dipping a cloth in dye to change its color. So these people testified to their changed heart regarding their sins.

7-10 But John saw many coming who were not ready to be baptized. The Pharisees were a religious party of Jews. Many years earlier they had formed this party and called themselves the Separated Ones. At first they determined to respect the Law of Moses, and to keep it from being destroyed by their enemies. There were about 6,000 Pharisees by John's time. But they had gradually put their own teachings above the word of God. They emphasized fastings, saying of prayers and giving to the poor; but they used these to cover over their wicked lives. They were very religious on the outside but their hearts were full of sin. In their pride they looked down on the other Jews. We will meet them often as we go through Matthew.

The Sadducees were mostly of a higher class of people and included some priests. But they were more of a political party who rejected the traditions of the Pharisees. They did not believe in resurrection nor angels nor any spirits.

When John saw these Pharisees and Sadducees coming to him, he had some very sharp words for them. "Snakes," he called them, "poisonous snakes"! Their teachings were contrary to God's Word. Their influence was deadly poison to Israel because they taught in the name of "religion." God's wrath was coming on them. The wrath of God is His rightful anger against sin. It was going to sweep over them like a flood. They should flee, run away, escape from it. But how could they? They had not come to confess their sins. Just to **say** they wanted to repent was not enough. They were religious Israelites, descendants of Abraham, and they thought that was good enough.

But pride in ancestors is empty pride. It is a false pillow to rest on. It is no credit to us if our grandfather lived a life of faith. We added nothing to his faith. We are responsible for our own lives. It was God who gave Abraham children. Isaac was born by a miracle of God, Hebrews 11.11,12. And God is able to turn stones into children of Abraham if He chooses to do so. See Genesis 18.14.

John warned them plainly that their lives must be changed. They must show by their actions that they had truly repented. They were like fruit trees which produced only leaves. If no good fruit came the owner would cut it down and the ax was already aimed at the roots, Matthew 7.16-20. The one who does not repent and turn from sin will be thrown into the fire of God's awful judgment. That was John's earnest warning to them and to us.

11,12 Then, in verses 11,12, John turned their and our attention to the coming King Himself. Salvation consists of turning **from** sin **to** the Savior. John will introduce this One to us later on, but here he tells us that He is coming and what He will be like. The coming King would be far greater than John. John was not worthy to untie or carry His sandals. The King is greater than any of His servants. Here are seven references to our Lord Jesus as the Greater One. Look up the references and fill in the blanks with who or what He is greater than:

        Matthew 12.6 _____
        Matthew 12.41 _____
        Matthew 12.42 _____
        John 4.12 _____

John 8.53 _____
Hebrews 6.13 _____
1 John 4.4 _____

John baptized with water, the baptism of Repentance. But only the coming King can regenerate, that is, give new life. He will baptize with the Holy Spirit and fire. The life-giving Spirit of God came at Pentecost, sent by our Lord Jesus as He had promised in John 16.7. In Acts 2.3 His coming was associated with fire. Fire is often linked with God's presence, as in Hebrews 12.29. Its action is to destroy the evil and purify the good, Malachi 3.2,3.

This is further illustrated in verse 12 in the work of the Harvester. On the threshing floor the grain is separated from the chaff and straw. The grain contains the life-germ. It pictures those who have eternal life through faith in Christ, John 3.16,36. But all who have not life in Christ are dead like straw and chaff, Psalm 1.4-6. All such will be burned in God's terrible judgment-fire that cannot be put out, Matthew 25.41,46; Revelation 14.10,11. Christ the King is the great Divider of mankind.

The King's Baptism, 3.13-17

Now at the age of 30 Jesus comes out of His quiet, hidden life at Nazareth in Galilee. He is about to begin His public service for about 3½ years. But before it begins He must go to see His herald, John the Baptizer. It seems He waited until all the other people had been baptized that day, Luke 3.21. Then He went up to John and asked him to baptize Him. This surprised John and he objected. He had been listening to all the people confessing and repenting of their sin. But John knew Jesus had no sin to confess. So he told Jesus, YOU should be baptizing me! He could not understand why Jesus wanted to confess and repent of sin because He had none, 1 Peter 2.22.

But Jesus was "born under the law to redeem those under the law," Galatians 4.4. He had come to fulfill the law, Matthew 5.17. He came to take the sinners' place of judgment in order to save them from their sins. Now He was taking the first step on the long road to the cross. There He will be the sinners' substitute, 2 Corinthians 5.21. Here He is taking the step of identification with sinners. Read Psalm 69.6 and Isaiah 53.6 and 12. Numbered with transgressors! What wonderful grace! How He loved us! Praise Him!

15 Jesus told John that it was the right thing for both of them to do.

It was right for John to baptize Jesus because He told him to do so. It was right for Jesus to be baptized so that He might perfectly fulfill the will of His Father. The Father sent the Son to be the Savior of the world, 1 John 4.14.

16 This was pleasing to the Father and the Holy Spirit. As soon as Jesus came up from the water the Spirit came on Him in the form of a dove. This was a sign to John that Jesus **was** the Son of God, John 1.32-34. Why did the Spirit take the form of a dove? Perhaps some Bible references to doves will help us to understand a little of the character of the Holy Spirit:

> Song of Solomon 2.14 — Modesty, beauty, sweet voice
> Song of Solomon 6.9 — Purity, (holiness)
> Matthew 10.16 — Innocent, blameless
> Genesis 8.11 — The peaceful one
> Isaiah 60.8 — The heavenly one
> Psalm 68.13 — The glorious one.

The coming of the Holy Spirit to rest on Jesus was like the anointing oil of the Old Testament. In Israel priests (Exodus 28.41), prophets (1 Kings 19.16) and kings (1 Samuel 9.16) were anointed. In each of these offices we see pictures of our Lord Jesus, Hebrews 4.14; Acts 3.22; Matthew 27.37; Revelation 19.16. Here our Lord Jesus was anointed, as it were, by the Holy Spirit for the fulfilling of all these offices as He began His public service. See also Psalm 45.7; Hebrews 1.9; Isaiah 11.1-5.

17 Now a Voice is heard from heaven. Not only is the Holy Spirit pleased with God the Son, so also is God the Father. Listen to His words:

> This is My Son — Testimony to the Deity of Jesus Christ. This reminds us of Psalm 2.7, *You are My Son!* Who would dare to deny this?
> Whom I Love — Infinite love—we cannot measure it. Compare Genesis 22.2 in Abraham's life.
> I am well pleased — Infinite delight—God's Son is the joy of heaven. Compare Isaiah 42.1.

In verse 15 we have the first words of the Lord Jesus recorded by Matthew. They are the key to the King's "life motto" on earth: Do the right thing before God, fulfill His will.

In verse 17 we have God the Father's response to that — full delight and satisfaction, publicly declared. God had been watching all those 30 years of "hidden" life of Jesus in Nazareth of Galilee. Of it all the Father says, I am well pleased with His every word, thought and deed!

Also the Father was well pleased with His Son's baptism as He, as it were, set His face toward the cross. *Therefore does My Father love Me because I lay down My life* . . . . John 10.17.

So we have found the Holy Trinity present at this important event. God the Son, together with God the Father and God the Spirit, begins His (and Their) public service in beautiful harmony and unity.

Chapter 4

The Testing of the King

1   The Spirit of God has just come upon Jesus (full of the Spirit, Luke 4.1). Immediately (Mark 1.12) He led Jesus to a wild desert place, perhaps in the desert of Judea. The purpose is important: to be tested by the devil. Before the King could reign He must be thoroughly tested as to His true character. To be the true King it must be proved that He is the true, perfect Man. He must be able to defeat His (and our) enemies.

The devil is the one who will test Him. In the Old Testament God used him to test Job, read Job 1 and 2. Here he is going to test the King Himself. This was not to find out if Jesus could sin (He could **not**!). But it was to prove that He could not sin. See 2 Corinthians 5.21 - *He knew no sin;* 1 Peter 2.22 - *He never committed sin;* 1 John 3.5- *In Him was no sin.* (see footnote below*)

2   For 40 days and nights Jesus was without food. By then He became very hungry. His whole body was crying out for nourishment. What a way to begin His public service! (We remember He closed His life on the cross being very thirsty, John 19.28). Very hungry and very thirsty! The Perfect Man keenly felt our human needs.

3   Luke 4.2 suggests that Satan was busy tempting Jesus during all those 40 days and nights. Now he seems to come with a final approach, making three direct, terrible attacks.

When Satan tempted Adam and Eve in the garden of Eden he used three attacks. 1 John 2.16 summarizes the three areas of both temptations:

1 John 2.16	Genesis 3	Matthew 4
bodily appetites (body)	Fruit of tree — good for food	Bread - feed your body
seeing, wanting (soul)	Pleasing to eyes	Show off - call attention to self
pride (of possessions) (spirit)	desirable/wisdom	Be ruler; be Number One

---

*Footnote: For more complete help on this question, see the book *Could God Incarnate Sin*, by D.B. Long. Published by Everyday Publications Inc.

2,3 Attack Number One: First Satan attacked at a time of physical weakness. He said, as it were, Put your body first, feed yourself. But God's order is: spirit first, soul next, and body last. See 1 Thessalonians 5.23. Satan said - Put yourself first. God says, Put God first, Deuteronomy 6.5; Matthew 22.37.

God the Father had declared openly that Jesus was His Son, chapter 3.17. Now Satan questioned that. He tried to put a big IF to it: IF you are God's Son. Then he tempted Jesus to prove His Sonship by turning stones into bread. Jesus was the all-powerful God and could very easily do so. He had fed many thousands of Israelites for 40 years in the desert, Exodus 16. But there was something more important than feeding His hungry body.

4 Defense Number One: God's Word is more important than daily bread. Jesus quoted from Deuteronomy 8.3. Israel had become hungry in the desert so that God could teach them that they needed every word of God, that is spiritual food.

Jesus is the Perfect Man and here tells Satan that He would obey His Father's word rather than feed His own body. It would be wrong to turn stones into bread if His Father had not told Him to do so. He would not act apart from His Father's command, John 8.28,29.

In this way Jesus used the Bible like the Sword of the Spirit (see Ephesians 6.17) to drive Satan back. This is an example to us. Satan is too strong and smart for us to defeat him. But we have God's Word —let's use it whenever Satan attacks us; he will go down defeated. Our true strength is this: not to push our own rights, but to submit to the will of God our Father.

5,6 Attack Number Two: Next the devil changed location and plan of attack. From the lonesome desert he took Jesus to the Holy City, Jerusalem, (Nehemiah 11.1; Isaiah 48.2; 52.1) to the top of the Holy temple. He also took the Old Testament Bible along. The devil can "turn religious" too. It is here he becomes even more dangerous to us. Jesus used the Bible to ward off the first attack, so Satan used the Bible this time to tempt Him to sin.

6 The point of the attack now is: Prove you trust God by jumping off this temple. Be a hero! IF you are God's Son He will protect you. Satan quoted from Psalm 91.11,12.

Now let's watch out when Satan quotes from the Bible. His agents are doing it every day. Teachers of false cults quote many verses from the Bible to "prove" their evil teachings. But they do just like their father, the Devil. He misquoted verses and left out part of them. You see, we must take the whole Bible in balance, and not take one verse out of its setting. We must study and compare them all.

Read what Satan said to Jesus in verse 6. Now turn to Psalm 91.11,12. Do you see what Satan left out? "In all your ways . . ." Proverbs 3.6 tells us to acknowledge the Lord in all our ways, that is, do HIS will. And Psalm 37.34 says that we keep the Lord's way by waiting on Him.

Then too, look back at Psalm 91 verse 13. Do you see why Satan didn't quote that verse to Jesus? The lion, snake and dragon are all pictures of Satan himself (see 1 Peter 5.8; Revelation 20.2). So that verse foretells that the One who depends on God and obeys Him will totally defeat Satan.

7 **Defense Number Two:** Notice the answer Jesus gives: "The Bible also says . . ." We must compare all scriptures. Every verse must be balanced with the rest of the Bible. So Jesus quoted from Deuteronomy 6.16 — Don't put the Lord to a foolish test by tempting Him. It is like taking His name in a joke. We are not to "play around" with our faith in God. We must not mock God by unbelieving challenges to His love. They only prove our own fear and unbelief.

Jesus, the true King "after God's own heart," never acted foolishly; He never put on a show to entertain people. The devil suggested that if Jesus jumped down safely everyone would believe He was the Son of God. But Jesus knew that if He jumped down it would only show that He did NOT fully obey His Father. So Satan was defeated again by the Sword of the Spirit.

8,9 **Attack Number Three:** The King has a rival king. Now in the final, desperate attack Satan comes out as his true, wicked self. What he really wants is the worship that belongs to God alone.

Place: on top of a very high mountain, we are not told where.

Plan: Show all the great, glorious kingdoms of the world. These were probably not Babylon, Egypt, Persia or Greece. They had all declined and faded away (because they had been under Satan's rule). But perhaps it was a rapid, instant (Luke 4.5) view of some still at the height of their glory: Rome, China, India, Parthians, Afghans, Mayans, Aztecs, and perhaps even future empires? Quickly Satan showed their glory but not their wickedness, weakness and destruction.

9 **Possession:** They belonged to Satan (see Luke 4.6). This is an amazing statement. Did Satan really have power over them all? Yes, the Bible clearly tells us so. Satan is called the god-ruler of this world, John 12.31; 14.30; 16.11; the prince of the power of the air, Ephesians 2.2; the authority over this dark world, Ephesians 6.12; the god of this age, 2 Corinthians 4.4. But how did Satan get power over the kingdoms of men?

Adam was made ruler over the earth by God, Genesis 1 and Psalm 8. But in Genesis 3 Satan tempted and deceived Eve in Eden. Adam was defeated by Satan and lost his rule. Satan snatched Adam's "crown" and took over his authority. Jesus did not dispute Satan's claim, but He had come to earth to defeat him, to destroy his works (1 John 3.8) and destroy him too (Hebrews 2.14).

Purpose: At this point in the temptation Satan proposes to Jesus: You may have all these kingdoms without doing battle. In one easy act you may become King of the earth. How?

Price: "Just bow down and worship me! Bow, admit they are mine, worship me and admit that I gave them to you, and they will all be yours." Just think! Satan was willing to give up all the kingdoms of the world for one moment of homage and worship by Jesus. (But Jesus valued the worth of one soul more than the whole world, Matthew 16.26).

In this way Satan tempted Jesus to take a "short cut" to the kingdom — the crown without the cross. But God's way is — first the cross then the crown; first suffering then reigning.

10,11 Defense Number Three: One more swift, clean cut from the Sword of the Spirit, from Deuteronomy 6.13: The Scripture says, Worship and serve the Lord God only. That's all it took to send the devil fleeing.

The True King — has conquered Satan — here in the desert
has condemned Satan — on the cross, John 12.31.
will throw Satan into the lake of fire in a coming day, Revelation 20.10.

Satan leaves the scene of battle. Jesus remains! The world and its desires pass away, but the Man who does the will of God lives and remains forever, 1 John 2.17. Jesus did not take the short-cut, He will go to the cross and take the kingdoms from Satan. Then later, He will come again to set up His kingdom on earth; we read, *The kingdom of the world has become the kingdom of our Lord and His Christ, and HE will reign forever and ever,* Revelation 11.15.

Then Matthew adds that angels came and took care of Jesus, that is, gave Him food, drink and strength. Compare Elijah in 1 Kings 19.6,7.

Lesson for us: A great Bible teacher wrote, "The enemy is proved unable to overcome **obedience** to the Word of God." David and great David's greater Son (Jesus) both could say, *I have set the LORD always before me . . . I will not be shaken,* Psalm 16.8.

May we, too, know true victory over Satan by total OBEDIENCE to our Lord God.

Matthew 4.10-22

The King Begins Public Service, 4.12-25

12   The King has been tested and proved to be "true gold." He has defeated His chief enemy. Now He can begin His public service. As He does so we read that His herald, John the Baptizer, has been put in prison. John's public work has ended and he sinks into the shadows as the King Himself takes up our full attention. We will meet John again in chapter 11.

13-16   In verses 13 to 16 we see the King returning to Galilee. But instead of living in Nazareth He takes up residence in Capernaum for the time being. Capernaum was a town on the north end of the Sea of Galilee, in the old tribal territories of Zebulun and Naphtali.

But why did He settle there? Once again Matthew brings out an "identity picture" reference from the Old Testament, Isaiah 9.1,2. There Galilee is described as being "of the Gentiles." It was the area which had been most overrun by foreign invaders. It was backward, weak and despised by Judeans. Galilee was where the **need** was greatest. Moral and spiritual **darkness** was **on** the people because it was **in** them. **Death** was the result of sin and darkness. No wonder Jesus went **there** to begin His preaching and teaching. The great Light dawned, the Light of the world, Jesus Himself, John 1.4; 8.12.

17   The Message of the King. He takes up where His herald, John, had left off. He confirmed and established it as God's message.

REPENT—As we have already seen, repentance is more than sorrow or shedding tears. It is more than religious penance of trying to "pay" for our sins. Repentance is a deep heart-change of attitude toward sin, self and God. It is a complete change of our direction, because we are wrong in our hearts.

The KINGDOM—We are wrong in our allegiance to Satan; his kingdom is the kingdom of darkness, Colossians 1.13.

OF HEAVEN—This is the new message:
    from a new Source — God;
    with new authority — from above;
    and new objective — heaven.

AT HAND, near — The King Himself has come down right to where we are.

18-22   **The Men of the Kingdom.** The King calls His first followers. They were not the noble, rich or mighty, but common men:

first Simon Peter and his brother Andrew, busy fishermen. Then the two sons of Zebedee, James and John, busy preparing nets.

Note the Royal Call: *COME* — Peter and Andrew evidently already knew Jesus and had trusted Him in John 1. Here they are called to service and discipleship.

FOLLOW — this meant obedience and submission to the King. The disciple was a learner who intended to follow.

ME— Jesus is the all-attractive Person. They did not join a cause, an organization or a movement. They were attracted to a Person. This is what Christianity is all about — it is CHRIST.

Instant results were:

        they left their nets — jobs, income
        they left their boats — possessions
        they left their father — family, dear ones

Mark 3.14 adds the purpose for calling the disciples: to be with HIM.

Here is a **Companionship**. Their best training and education was to be with Him. *Learn of Me*, Matthew 11.29.

It includes **Consecration**. That is dedication to the King's interests, giving ourselves wholly to Him, Romans 12.1-2.

It involves **Creation.**"I will *make* you." He will shape and use the abilities we lay at His feet.

Then will come **Commission**. "He sent them out," 10.5; 28.19,20.

23-25 The Power of the King. Jesus began traveling all through Galilee, the needy district. (1) He **taught** the Word of God in the Jewish synagogues, or churches. He used Old Testament Scripture, as in Luke 4.16-21.(2) He **preached** the Good News about His kingdom and Himself, the King. (3) He **healed** all the sick people. So He reached their hearts, minds and bodies. There is no part of mankind that He cannot touch and bless.

Naturally the news about this wonderful Person rapidly spread throughout the whole countryside of Syria. All kinds of sick persons were brought to Him — (1) mental patients, epileptics; (2) spiritual needs, demon-possessed; and (3) bodily sicknesses, those suffering pain and paralysis. The Royal Power of Jesus was sufficient to heal them all. Then huge crowds came from farther away even from as far as Jerusalem.

Chapter 5

The Laws of the Kingdom
Chapters 5-7

The Blessings of the Kingdom, 5.1-12

1,2 We often read that when Jesus looked on the great crowds of people He had compassion on them, as Chapter 14.14. He knew their need, they were like sheep without a shepherd. He is the great King-Shepherd who came to meet their need and to bless them. The King now begins to tell His disciples what His kingdom will be like. It is going to be entirely different from any other kingdom. He begins with

The Character of the Citizens, 5.3-12

The very first word He uses is *Blessed*. This was a well known word to the Jewish people. In their Bible. the Old Testament, the terms *Bless, Blessed* and *Blessing* occur over 350 times. It is a rich word meaning happy, favored or content. The blessed person knows perfect peace, joy and rest in his heart. It is found in such well-known verses as Psalm 1.1; 2.12; 32.1,2. You can easily find many other references.

The King begins by describing the citizens of His Kingdom. But we can scarcely read these verses 3 to 12 without realizing they really describe the King Himself. What a beautiful picture of

The Character of the King:

1. *Poor in spirit.* He was the rich One who became poor for us, 2 Corinthians 8.9. He was the High One who took the low place for us, Philippians 2.5-8.

2. *The Mourner.* To mourn means to feel deep grief or sorrow. Who ever felt grief and sorrow more deeply than Jesus did? He is called the Man of Sorrows, familiar with suffering, Isaiah 53.3. He wept in John 11, Luke 19 and Hebrews 5. Find the verses in those chapters and notice for whom He wept.

3. *The Meek or Gentle, Humble One.* Meekness must never be confused with weakness. There is no connection! Meekness is really strength which has been taught to submit, like the mighty ox trained to pull the yoke in humble obedience to its master. Jesus refers to this in Matthew 11.28,29.

4. *Intense Desire for the Right.* Hunger and thirst speak of great desire. As we saw in chapter 4.6,8, Jesus did not desire fame or earthly glory. Instead He only wanted to do the right, His Father's will, John 4.34; Psalm 40.6-8.

5. *Merciful.* He was moved with kindness, compassion to needy ones, 9.36. He left heaven to meet us in our need, Luke 5.13; 10.33; 23.34.

6. *Pure in Heart.* Pure means clean. But it also includes "with the whole heart, holding nothing back" from God. Jesus was not only without sin (remember notes on chap. 4.1?) but He was also totally loyal to His Father, John 8.29. He had no wrong motives or ambitions.

7. *Peacemaker.* Christ made peace, not peace at any price but peace at great price, Ephesians 2.14,15; Colossians 1.20. One Bible teacher has said that the world has lots of peace-breakers and peace-fakers; Christians are peace-takers; but the only Peace Maker is our King of Peace.

8. *Persecuted for the cause of Right.* Jesus was hated, persecuted and murdered because the darkness hates the light, John 3.19-21; 15.18-20.

9. *Insulted and Mocked.* Read Isaiah 53. Think about Matthew 26.67; and 27.26-31. Yet He rejoiced to do His Father's will, John 15.11; 17.13.

But now let's look at the character of this King's subjects. We have noted that the King is different (far greater) than any other king. His subjects are different than men's ideas of greatness and success. So the kingdom will be and is different than all other kingdoms.

Usually men think of a kingdom in terms of power, wealth and glory: mighty armies and navies and missiles; successful commerce and manufacturing; proud ruler and prosperous citizens. For the Jews of Jesus' time it meant an earthly king with power enough to defeat and drive out the Roman armies and become independent.

Jesus' disciples shared this hope as they looked for an earthly kingdom, Acts 1.6. They must have been greatly surprised as they heard Jesus tell what His kingdom would be like. He does not outline a military program. He does not suggest they take Jerusalem by storm. They were not to kill king Herod or Pilate the Governor. Nothing of the kind! He does not begin with the earthly but the **spiritual**.

Character is more important than conquering armies. Right is better than Might. Man's spiritual life must be right before material things can be made right. What is internal and eternal outweighs the external. Christ's kingdom is of heaven and it is personal, inside the hearts of His followers, Luke 17.21.

In the future Christ is going to reign over the whole world and every knee will bow to Him. But now His kingdom is where He rules in individual hearts and lives. This is illustrated in the life of king David, 1 Samuel 22.1,2. David was anointed king over Israel, but he spent years in hiding. He was rejected, hated and persecuted, but a few people (400) followed him and were faithful to him. They suffered with him and later reigned with him when God gave him the throne of Israel.

Now let's consider in detail what the true followers of the great King are like. There are nine characteristics. These are like the nine-fold fruit of the Spirit in Galatians 5.22,23. See if you can connect some of the ideas.

1. *Blessed are the poor in spirit,* v. 3. As we have noted, Jesus begins with what is spiritual. It is the first, most important part of man, 1 Thessalonians 5.23. But it is the most neglected by man. Jesus said that true blessedness is associated with recognizing our spiritual need. "I am poor and needy," wrote David in Psalm 40.17. The poor, needy, empty heart cries to God, Psalm 34.6. It is the humble cry of weakness and dependence. The beggar, without any good thing, is willing to come and bow before this King:

> *Nothing in my hand I bring;*
> *Simply to Your cross I cling;*
> *Naked, come to You for dress;*
> *Helpless, look to You for grace.*
> *Foul, I to the Fountain fly,*
> *Wash me, Savior, or I die!*

The proud, self-sufficient, self-righteous, "rich" one is sent away empty, Luke 1.53, Mark 10.24. But the kingdom of heaven is for the poor in spirit. This is the first step to receiving that kingdom. Have you taken it?

2. *Blessed are those who mourn,* v.4. Solomon wrote that it is better to go to the house of mourning than to a house of feasting; sorrow is better than laughter, Ecclesiastes 7.2-4. Of course the men of this world think just the opposite. "Let's eat, drink and be merry," they sing. But the end of such men is death, Proverbs 14.12.

Jesus said that happiness, blessedness, comes to those who mourn for their sins. Fools make a mock of sin, Proverbs 14.9, but happy is the one who confesses and forsakes sin, Proverbs 28.13,14. Mourning brings tears of repentance, Psalm 119.136. This is the next sure step to receiving the kingdom of God, 2 Corinthians 7.10. The result: they shall be comforted. What a comfort to know my sins are forgiven, Matthew 9.2. Then to know the Comforter-Helper of God, the Holy Spirit, as my daily Companion, John 14.16-18. Does our reader enjoy this blessedness?

3. *Blessed are the meek, humble, gentle*, v.5. Men of the world think that success and wealth come only to the proud, pushy, self-confident people. These stand up for their rights and crush all who oppose them; they get the position of power and control. Jesus taught just the opposite. Great ones in His kingdom must take the low place, chapter 20.25-28. Here He says the blessed-happy ones are the gentle, meek ones. (Look again at the previous note on verse 5). He was the meekest yet the all-powerful One. He humbled Himself in obedience to His Father. So must we.

The reward is "shall inherit the land." Israel was given an earthly inheritance, the promised land—Canaan. Believers in our Lord Jesus today look for a spiritual inheritance. Heaven is our home, John 14.1-3. This includes all the spiritual blessings which are ours by faith in Christ, Ephesians 1.3, Hebrews 11.13-16.

4. *Blessed are those who hunger and thirst for righteousness*, v.6. When we are starving for food and thirsting for water we can only think about food and water. These intense desires drive out any others. This is true physically but much more so spiritually. Jesus said that blessedness comes to those who greatly desire to do what is right in God's eyes. First, this means being right with God, having salvation, justification through faith in Christ, Romans 4.23-25; then, living our daily lives in the right way, pleasing to Him, Matthew 6.33.

Do you put this first in your life? Is your spiritual appetite keen and sharp? If so, you have already experienced the last word in this verse—filled or satisfied. See John 4.1-26; 7.37-40.

5. *Blessed are the merciful*, v.7. The merciful are those who care; they show compassion and kindness to the undeserving. Our King is **full** of mercy, He delights in mercy, Luke 6.36. He is rich in mercy, Ephesians 2.4. He stood firmly against sin but He was quick to show mercy to the guilty. See John 8.1-11. Members of His kingdom will show mercy and lovingkindness. Forgiving others is a sign of having received mercy. We will see more of this in chapter 18.

6. *Blessed are the pure in heart*, v.8. When Jesus speaks of the heart He is not referring to the organ in our bodies which pumps the blood. The heart speaks of the central, innermost part of us, called self, the "I" who lives inside the body. It is the "inner man" who decides what we do and say. We think with our minds, we feel with our emotions but we rule our lives by our will. Our heart, our very self, is unclean with sin, Jeremiah 17.9; Mark 7.20-23. Sin keeps us away from God. *Depart from me for I am a sinful man O Lord,* Luke 5.8.

The blessed-happy person is he or she who cries to God, *Create in me a pure heart, O Lord,* Psalm 51.10. If we confess our sin He will purify us from all sin, 1 John 1.9. Those who are members of this kingdom are pure in heart, with no make-believe mask trying to hide sin. They will see God—they will discover Him and understand Him.

7. *Blessed are the peacemakers,* v.9. God is the God of peace, Romans 15.33. Jesus is the Prince of peace, Isaiah 9.6. He is the true peacemaker, Ephesians 2.15,16. His kingdom is made up of righteousness, peace and joy in the Holy Spirit, Romans 14.17. If we are members of that kingdom we should show His character and do His work in our daily situations. We should live at peace with our neighbors, not paying back wrongs or being full of revenge. Read Romans 12.17-21. God calls such people His sons, grown up and mature. Such persons honor Him.

8. *Blessed are those who are persecuted for doing what is right,* v.10. Our King suffered for doing what was right, 1 Peter 2.21-23. He warns us that if we belong to Him the world will hate and persecute us also, John 15.18-21; 2 Timothy 3.12. If we suffer for doing the right thing this is pleasing to God, 1 Peter 2.20. The kingdom belongs to us.

9. *Blessed are those who suffer for the name of Jesus,* vs. 11,12. To rejoice when this happens to us is a true sign of being members of Christ's kingdom. In Acts 5.17-42 the apostles experienced this and they were full of joy, v.41. So have thousands of others. Perhaps some of our readers are saying "Amen, it is true!"

. . . .

There are many examples in the Bible of believers who showed the above qualities in their lives. We will list one for each, and the reader can try to find others:

1.	Poor in spirit	Lazarus in Luke 16
2.	Mourner	Martha & Mary — John 11
3.	Meek, gentle	Moses — Numbers 12
4.	Righteousness	Timothy — 2 Timothy 3.15-17
5.	Merciful	David — 1 Samuel 24
6.	Pure in heart	Daniel — Daniel 1
7.	Peacemaker	Abraham — Genesis 13
8,9.	Persecuted/suffering	Stephen — Acts 7

So the King has given us this brief sketch of what members of His kingdom are like, and thus what His kingdom will be like. How do **you** fit into this picture?

Two Illustrations — Salt and Light, 5.13-16

Character is what counts in this kingdom. What we are will shape what we do. To influence others for good we must live out His life. The King now tells His followers:

You are the Salt of the Earth, 5.13

Salt was and is a very common and well known part of daily life. Why does the King use it to describe His followers? Their character was like salt in several ways:

1. Salt was a picture of judgment. In Genesis 19.26 Lot's wife was judged by God. She turned into a pillar of salt for her disobedience. This tells us that we should be careful to judge sin in our lives before God has to do so, 1 Corinthians 11.31,32.

2. Salt was an important part of Old Testament sacrifices, Leviticus 2.12,13. It was linked with suffering which would be the portion of the King's followers as we just saw in verses 10-12.

3. Salt was also linked with a covenant. Number 18.19 refers to the everlasting covenant of salt before the Lord. 2 Chronicles 13.5 also refers to this. In Bible lands a covenant or agreement was "signed" by both parties together tasting some salt. In fact we understand the Arabic word for salt is the same as for treaty. So the King's followers must realize they are in covenant relationship with Him.

4. Salt has healing and cleansing qualities. Compare 2 Kings 2.19-22 and Ezekiel 16.4. It was used in binding up wounds to make them heal, Isaiah 61.1. So believers' lives should have a healing influence on people around them, healing spiritual wounds and diseases.

5. Salt also was used to preserve foods. In hot climates without modern refrigeration salt is still used to prevent food from spoiling. The presence of Christians on earth today is holding off the total ruin of human society. When the Lord comes to take His people to heaven, this poor world will completely fall apart morally, spiritually and politically. Read 2 Thessalonians 2.5-12. Today believers are to live wholesome, clean lives in this wicked, corrupt society around.

6. Salt gives seasoning to our food and makes it taste better. Our lives and conversation are to be attractive to unbelievers, to help make them hungry and thirsty to know our King for themselves. They will desire the joy, peace and satisfaction that believers enjoy. Look up Colossians 4.6.

7. But there is a warning note also. Salt can lose its flavor, its saltiness. Some Christians lose their saltiness because they have lost their first love to Christ, see Revelation 2.4 and 3.16. Believers drift away from their love to the Lord and become useless to God and man. How many of these salt characteristics can you trace in your life?

Matthew 5.13-19

You are the Light of the World 5.14-16

14-16 In John 8.12 our Lord said, "I am the Light of the world." His disciples are to follow Him and walk in His light, 1 John 1.7. Now, while He is absent, John 9.5, His followers are lights, to let His light shine out through us.

Light clearly reveals everything, Ephesians 5.8-14. Believers are children of light. We are to be active witnesses for our Lord to the whole world. Two pictures are given:

1. A city on a hill cannot be hid. This suggests our witness as citizens of the heavenly city and kingdom. Together we have been "raised up" in Christ, Ephesians 2.6. This is what the "hill" may illustrate, Ephesians 1.3. Because we are "in Christ" and He is "in us," the city—of God—cannot be hid. Like lights we are to show His praises, 1 Peter 2.9.

2. A lamp would speak of our individual witness. Its purpose is to give light to everyone in the house. Wherever we live, work or worship, we are meant to let Christ's light shine through us.

But there is a warning here also. We are not to hide our lamp under a bowl or basket. This suggests letting things of earth—business, pleasure, etc.—crowd out our witness for our King. (Mark 4 adds a bed which suggests a life of ease and laziness. This also must not hinder our testimony for Christ.) Read 1 Thessalonians 5.5-8.

16 How do we let our light shine out? By living lives pleasing to the King, obeying His commands. People will recognize that we belong to our Father in heaven and they will give Him praise.

Where is your lampstand? Is your lamp in its place there? Is it burning brightly? Consider how John the Baptizer was a burning and shining light for his Lord, John 5.35.

The Authority of the King, 5.17-48

And now the King declares His supreme authority in the rest of this chapter and chapter 6. Notice ten times He says, *I tell you,* and four times, *I tell you the truth.* Let's look at each of these:

17-19 Verses 17-19 speak of the Old Testament Law. Jesus did not come to do away with the Law of Moses or the teachings of the old Prophets. They were God's message to Israel and could not be brushed aside. He came to fulfill them, to make them come true.

1. Part of the Old Testament was Divine instructions. The Jews called this the Torah. These were only a partial revelation, Hebrews 1.1,2. Jesus completed that revelation.

2. The prophets were also telling about future things. Jesus came to fulfill or bring to pass things foretold about Him. Over 20 times Matthew writes, "that it might be fulfilled what was written."

3. Moral rules in the Law and Prophets are given **full** meaning by Jesus. We will see this in the following verses.

18 (1) In verse 18 is the first time: I *tell you the truth*. The Law will stand and will not fail even until heaven and earth pass away. In our English language the smallest letter is *i*, and the smallest mark is the dot on the *i*. Jesus says that not one dot of an *i* will be done away with or disappear, but all will be fulfilled. So important are the Old Testament Scriptures. The ceremonial law (of offerings, feast days, circumcision, etc.) was all fulfilled and put away by Christ. But the moral law (regarding love to God and to mankind) stands today and forever. Not a dot of an *i* will ever be lost.

20 (2) I *tell you*—heaven's kingdom requires more right living than that of religious persons—scribes and Pharisees. They were very religious but it was all on the outside like whitewash or paint. Jesus called them **hypocrites**, they were pretending but not living according to God's way. (Compare Matthew 23.27,28). They did not measure up to His standard, Romans 3.23. Neither can we in our own strength, but a Christian is born again to new life. He is made right with God through faith in the Lord Jesus Christ, John 3.3,5,7; Romans 4.22-25.

21-24 The Old Testament Law said, *Do not murder*, Exodus 20.13. To kill someone brings punishment.

(3) *But I tell you*. Jesus looks deep into the heart. He says that anger and hatred are sins which will be judged. Even hatefully calling a brother a "good-for-nothing" will be judged by the court. And anyone hatefully calling a brother in Christ a **worthless fool** will be in danger of the lake of fire. This shows how serious word-sins are. Words can be as deadly as knives or guns, Matthew 12.36,37.

23,24 So in verses 23 and 24 Jesus warns against trying to worship God while having hatred in our hearts toward another person. We must be right with our fellow-men before God will accept our worship. There is no use in trying to bless God after cursing a man, James 3.9-12.

25,26 Verses 25 and 26 continue this. Jesus warns us to get right with our neighbor before he takes us to court. Once in court it will be too late. We suggest this pictures our relationship with God. Our sins demand death, Romans 6.23. But we should receive the Lord Jesus as our Savior. Then God will "settle out of court" before the judgment day, Romans 5.1; 8.1.

(4) I *tell you the truth*, v.26. At judgment day it will be too late, Revelation 20.11-15.

27-30 Again the Old Testament said, *Do not commit adultery*, Exodus 20.14. Sexual sin, either before marriage or after, was forbidden and punished in the Old Testament.

(5) But I *tell you*: adultery of heart through the eyes is the same as the physical sinful act. Again Jesus is looking into the **heart**. A bad thought is the same as a bad deed! Well do children sing, "Be careful, little eyes, what you see." Adults need to take care also.

Verse 30 gives a severe remedy: pluck out the eye, cut off the hand. We suggest this means more than the physical act. Later, in the Epistles, believers are taught to put to death our sinful acts, Romans 8.13, Colossians 3.5. We are to judge ourselves, now, day by day. Then we will not be judged in the coming day of judgment.

31,32 Divorce is next. The Old Testament taught that divorce was permissible for certain causes, Deuteronomy 24.1-4.

(6) *But I tell you*: divorce by husband causes adultery by wife and second husband at their second marriage. The exception is if the divorce was because of marital unfaithfulness on the part of the wife. This is a difficult subject. This verse is only one of many which deal with divorce. They must all be read and compared for a right view of this very important subject. See Footnote*

33-37 Oaths or vows versus truthfulness. The Old Testament demanded that a vow must be kept, Numbers 30.2, Deuteronomy 23.21. But the Pharisees were teaching that only oaths or vows linked with the temple were binding, Matthew 23.16-22.

(7) *But I tell you*, v.34, Do not use vows at all! Swearing and using oaths are not necessary for a believer, and are really from the evil one, Satan. They are a sad confession that our word, yes or no, is not dependable, James 5.12. Jesus always spoke of the simple, plain truth. He needed no oath to assure us of His truthfulness. His followers should do as He did. Look at Matthew 12.36.

38,39 The Pharisees explained the Old Testament Law to mean that one should pay back any wrong done to him. If someone hit him on the cheek he should hit him back on his cheek (only harder, to teach him a lesson!). However, in saying this they were overlooking another verse in the Law. Look up Leviticus 19.18. Many people today live by the rule of revenge: always get even!

---

*Footnote: Space does not allow more details here. The reader may be helped by the booklets, *A Biblical History of Marriage, Divorce and Remarriage* or *Fornication and Divorce*, published by Everyday Publications Inc.

(8) *But* I *tell you*, v.38: Do not take personal revenge. See Romans 12.19.

(We must note this verse does not teach what is called Pacifism, that is, that nations should lay down their weapons and not protect themselves. Romans 13.1-4 teaches that government is God's agent for keeping law and order, and for punishing criminals. This means there is need for police and armies. When our King comes again to rule over the whole world He will rule justly and THEN there will be peace and safety.)

But these verses refer to the individual revenge on a personal enemy. Believers are to suffer wrong and not try to "get even".

39   If a big bully hits you, give him another chance on the other cheek.

40   If you are taken to court, pay more than the law demands, not less.

41   If you are forced to go a mile, go two!

42   If a beggar asks for a piece of bread, give him two. Don't turn him away even if he is a "professional beggar." Give him bread plus the Bread of Life, the Word of God.

43,44   The Pharisees limited Old Testament love to friends. Then they wrongly added "hate your enemies."

(9) *But* I *tell you*: Love your enemies. For an example see Luke 10.30-37.

45   Then He gives us the true standard of measure: **God's** love. His love is for all; it is to the criminal as well as to the citizen who keeps the law. It is plentiful, His sunshine and rain is on everyone's garden alike. It is free, we cannot buy His love nor deserve it in any way. It is perfect.

46-48   Verses 46 to 48 sum up the chapter. The King's people are to be perfect, mature. Love is the key to all the above instructions. Go back over all nine sections of this chapter and write down how LOVE is the real key that fits each problem.

To return evil for evil is to be like an animal.

To return evil for good is to be like the devil.

To return good for good is to be like humans.

To return good for evil is to be like God Himself.

Chapter 6

The Laws of the Kingdom (cont'd)

The King next challenges His people to be real, sincere in their hearts. He flashes a threefold warning light before us: Watch out, take heed, be careful. Three times He warns against doing things just to be seen by men: doing religious good deeds, v.1; saying prayers, v.5; and fasting, v.16.

Giving to the Poor

2 (10) I *tell you the truth*: They have received their reward in full.
Who? Those who blow the trumpet and make a big show when they give money to the poor. They do it to be honored by men, v.2. They are praised and honored by their neighbors. But there will be no reward in heaven because they already received the praise they worked for, from men. They were "acting" before men and they got the actor's handclap.

True followers of the King will give in secret. No one else will know except One, our Father in heaven. He sees everything that is "secret" and will reward in heaven. See verses 19-21.

Prayer

5 (11) I *tell you the truth*: They have received their reward in full.
Who? Those who love to stand in churches and on street corners, praying to be seen by men. That is as far as their prayer reaches—to men. It never reaches heaven. Their aim is to sound good to men. But the King tells His people to pray in secret. We are to go into our private room and close the door. No man can see through a closed door so no man will praise us (nor disturb us). But God sees and hears the secret prayer, and He will answer, v.6. That is the first rule of prayer.

7 The next rule is: don't repeat long, empty phrases over and over and over. Pagans do this because they think they can get their god's attention that way. Find where this is illustrated in 1 Kings 18 and in Acts 19. Write the references in your Bible.

8 Prayer is not a recital of our needs and burdens to God. He knows our needs long before we even have them. Some people pray long prayers telling God all about things He already knows.

9 Well then, how should we pray? What is prayer? In verses 9-13 the King gives us a pattern for our praying. It is often called the Lord's Prayer, but that really is in John 17. This one is better called the Disciple's Prayer. Many believers (and unbelievers) say this prayer word for word in unison at churches every week. But this easily becomes what Jesus just described in verse 7—meaningless repetition. Also He has just told His followers that they should pray in private, secretly, v.6. Then too, we notice that Luke 11.2-4 gives us this prayer in a different form. All of this leads us to believe that the Lord is telling us HOW to pray and not WHAT to pray. In other words, it is a pattern with important principles to follow, but not a formal, word-for-word ritual to be repeated endlessly. So let's briefly note those principles.

1. It is a family prayer. Only believers (members of the King's family) can speak to God as "our Father." So it is a personal prayer to a dearly loved Father.

2. It recognizes the greatness of God—He is in the heavens. The Bible speaks of three heavens: (1) air, where birds fly, Luke 9.58 lit.; (2) starry heavens, Matthew 24.29; and (3) third heaven, dwelling place of God, 2 Corinthians 12.2. Our great God is in all three at the same time! 1 Kings 8.27. He is not only far away but He is also as near to us as our breath.

3. It reminds us of the holiness of God and of His Name. His Name is sacred. We are to honor and respect it at all times.

10 It teaches the necessity of putting important things first. In verse 9 it was His Name. Here it is His Kingdom and His Will. His kingdom is present already in the hearts of His followers, as we have already seen. We pray for the day when He will come and reign over all creatures: **Even so, come Lord Jesus!**

His will is the most important thing in the life of His true followers. We should seek to know what His will is for every day of our lives.

Teach me Your way, O Lord,
Not my will but Yours —today.

God's will should be central in our prayers. This is the measure of heaven on earth for our lives.

11   First we put God in His rightful place in our thinking; then we begin to make our requests—not until then. Daily needs include: (1) daily food for our body. He cares for and loves us. We do not pray in order to tell Him about our needs—He already knows them. But He loves to hear His children tell Him how much we need Him.

12   We also need (2) daily forgiveness for our daily sins. This is very important to all believers—cleansing, 1 John 1.7-2.2.

13   (3) Deliverance from testing. Satan is always trying to trip us up, Luke 22.31. We need daily deliverance from the Evil One. Only our mighty King is greater than Satan, so we need HIS saving and keeping power daily—His safety.

14,15   Verses 14 and 15 warn us that we should be forgiving to those who wrong us; if not, we can hardly expect our Father to forgive us.

Some old Bibles add a note of victory and faith: *Yours is the Kingdom and power and glory forever.* That is what prayer is all about. And that is what this book by Matthew is all about.

Fasting, 6.16-18

16   (12) *I tell you the truth*: They have received their reward in full.

Who? Those who show off to people that they are going without food. In Old Testament days fasting took place at times of sorrow and distress, as 1 Samuel 1.7; times of national trouble and repentance, as Nehemiah 9.1. In the New Testament the Pharisees used to mark their faces with ashes and leave their hair untidy and put on long faces—all to call attention to themselves. This was so men would praise them for being so "religious." Men did praise them so that was their reward. If you want to know how GOD felt about their fasting and Old Testament fasting, study Isaiah 58 carefully.

17,18   The King told His followers not to let anyone know when they were fasting. They were to have bright, clean faces and hair brushed. Joy not sadness was to be on their faces. Again the Father sees in secret and will reward.

Treasures in Heaven, 6.19-24

The King now (vs. 19-34) teaches how His followers should handle earthly things, such as money, food, clothing. First of all, what should be our attitude toward money? The King tells us to store it up—save it! But we have to choose **where** we will put it. He tells us that earth is not a safe place to keep our treasures. The moth eats clothing. Rust eats metal. Thieves can steal both. Riches have a habit of flying away as if on wings, Proverbs 23.5. Earthly possessions lose value by wearing out, rotting away, rusting, getting out of date, or stolen. (How rich would **you** be if a bomb destroyed your city or country? What would you have left?)

But the "Bank of Heaven" is totally safe. We can put our money and time and talents to work for the Lord and this is the way to deposit them safely in the eternal bank of heaven. No enemies can destroy or steal. On earth death is the final thief. When we die we leave everything we own, see 1 Timothy 6.7. But in heaven there will be no death, no destruction, no loss. So the King's word to us is to invest all we can in the Eternal Savings Bank of Heaven, Hebrews 13.5,6.

22,23 But we need the right kind of vision to do this. We see with the eyes of our body. When our eyes are healthy our whole body will be full of light. But a diseased eye can keep the light out (blindness). Or it can cause a bad picture of what we are looking at. In 2 Peter 1.9 we read about being short-sighted. Many believers are too near-sighted spiritually. They only look at earthly, material things, and not at the heavenly, far-off things, which are eternal. Hold a small coin close to your eye and it will blot out the whole sky. In the same way, think only of money and wealth and it will be easy to forget that heavenly things are more important, and eternal. We should live our lives for our Lord and King, with eternity's values in view.

24 We have to choose between two masters. In Bible days there were many slaves. But a slave could belong to only one master and serve him. If we save up all our money on earth we are slaves to money. That is we live to get all the nice things money can buy for us. We are ruled by money and the love of money, see 1 Timothy 6.10. But we are serving God when we save up our money in heaven. We have to choose whom to serve. *As for me and my household we will serve the Lord,* said Joshua, *but you must choose for yourselves whom you are going to serve,* Joshua 24.15. How about you?

Worry about Food and Clothes, 6.25-34

25 (13) *I tell you the truth*—do not worry about food or clothing.

Now the King speaks about our attitude toward our daily needs. Six times He mentions **worry**—that means to be anxious, stay awake nights. Followers of our great King do not need to worry.

1. **Worry is unnecessary** to children of such a Father-God, vs 25,26. This does not mean we are not to take thought about providing for ourselves and our families. Nor that we are not to plan for them, 1 Timothy 5.8. But it does mean that we are not to take **anxious** thought. Our Father provides food for the birds. They do not have to plant seeds and harvest crops. But they **do** have to gather the food from where God puts it for them. If you watch birds you know that they are constantly busy looking for and finding food. God does not just drop it into their mouths. We, citizens of the Kingdom, are responsible to work to earn our living, 1 Timothy 5.8. See if you can find verses in 1 Thessalonians 4 and 2 Thessalonians 3 which tell us this.

2. **Worry is unworthy** of subjects of such a King, vs. 28-30.

29 (14) I *tell you*, All the beautiful royal robes of king Solomon could not compare with the lovely beauty of the wild flowers in the mountains and fields, because God made them. How much more beautifully does He clothe His people! He has clothed us with the garments of Salvation, Isaiah 61.10, and of Praise, 61.3. He will surely clothe our bodies with the dress or coat we may need today.

31,32 Unbelievers are always running after **things**—clothes, cars, houses, etc. We who are Christ's followers are to seek first and always HIS kingdom, the things of heaven. Then all these necessary things will be thrown in as well. Put God first in your life and everything else will fall into place properly.

34 3. **Worry is unfruitful** to us who are creatures of today. Who, by worrying, can add a single hour to his life or a few inches (centimeters) to his height? v.27. Who can change tomorrow by worry? v.34. Faith **trusts** God; worry **doubts** God. Faith lives one day at a time. It lives today in the light of Eternity.

By faith believers can sing

We praise God for all that is past
And we trust Him for all that is to come.

Chapter 7

The Laws of the Kingdom (cont'd)

Finding Fault in Others, 7.1-6

1,2 Followers of the King are not to judge others. Here judging has the meaning of finding fault, being critical. You are using every means to find some little fault in your brother? You may expect others to do the same to you. You measure out heaping spoonfuls of the bitter medicine of sharp criticism? You will surely have some of the same returned to you.

3-5 How dare you do that when you are not perfect yourself? In fact, you may think the speck of sawdust in your brother's eye is so bad, but you first need to take the big plank or log out of your own eye. The King calls you a hypocrite, a play-actor.

These are hard words but very necessary. One of the saddest sins among believers today is the proud, self-righteous attitude of fault-finding. It is so easy to see another's failures and faults and then to excuse or cover up the same faults in ourselves. The first place to begin looking for faults is in the mirror!

6 But we do need to use wisdom to tell the difference between believers and non-believers. Dogs and pigs are not very nice words to use about people. But those who have turned away from the Lord are ungodly and unclean, see 2 Peter 2.22 (read the whole chapter). We are told not to give them the precious jewels (truths) concerning the church and her blessings in Christ. They only despise and hate what is sacred and holy. But where can we find the wisdom to know the difference? In the following verses.

Prayer, 7.7-12

Our King urges us to do three things as we pray:

7,8 (1) **Ask.** This simply means to beg, in humble dependence and need. It is coming to the King with empty hands, saying, "I have nothing with which to buy what I need." He knows our need but wants us to exercise our faith. He longs to enrich us when we ASK. But we must ask with right motives, not just to get something for self, James 4.2,3, but to glorify our Lord's name.

(2) **Seek,** or **search.** This speaks of coming with care and diligence. We must be very definite in what we ask for. We search for specific things, Luke 15.4,8. In Acts 12.5 the church was praying earnestly to God for **Peter** and in verse 14 they received the definite answer. Perhaps too often we ask God for nothing (specific) and we get just that!

(3) **Knock** and keep on knocking until the answer comes. Keep at it and don't give up, Luke 18.1-8. In Colossians 4.12 Epaphras was always wrestling in prayer for the believers at Colosse.

The words really mean: keep on asking, keep on searching, keep on knocking, and the answers will keep on coming. We will be receiving, finding, and opening.

9-11 How much greater is our heavenly Father's love than any earthly father! God loves His needy children and longs to give them all the wisdom, strength and blessing they need. He spared not His Son, how will He not also with Him freely, graciously, lovingly give us all things? Romans 8.32. Blessed be His Name.

12 The King briefly sums up the Old Testament Law and Prophets.

This verse is often called the Golden Rule and some people think they can be saved by keeping it. But it is not a rule of life for unsaved people. The Law of Moses said we should love our neighbors as ourselves. But we are not able to do this (review chapter 5.19,20). It is only after we are born anew, through faith in Christ, that we can do so. It is only in His strength that we can live His life, Philippians 4.13.

The Final Appeal, 7.13-27

The King closes this Sermon on the Mount with an appeal to follow Him. He uses three illustrations to help us know what all this means.

1. All men are travelers, but there are two ways to go, vs. 13,14.
2. All men are producers—like fruit trees—but there are two kinds of fruit, vs. 15-23.
3. All men are builders, but there are two kinds of foundations, vs. 24-26. Let's look at each of these pictures.

People are travelers, 7.13,14

There are two gates leading to two road and two destinies. The narrow gate is hard to enter and the road beyond it is narrow and difficult. Only few people travel on it. But this road leads to LIFE, eternal life. What makes it so hard? You must turn aside from the big crowds in repentance for your sins. Turning away from sin is not easy. Confessing you are a sinner and trusting Christ as your Savior is not easy. It takes courage and faith. The gate is narrow so we can only enter one by one. We must personally bow to the King and trust Him. And He tells us plainly the road ahead is not easy. People will hate you, Satan will fight against you. You will suffer and may even be put to death. Look again at chapter 5:10-12 notes, also chapter 16.21-26, and Revelation 2.9-11. But what is at the end of the road? LIFE, and all the full meaning of abundant, eternal, joyful life in Christ, with Him and like Him in heaven forevermore. How wonderful!

But the wide gate and easy road are well traveled. Most people are on it and they think all is well because "everybody else" is going along that way too. But read Proverbs 14.12. The end of that road is death and destruction.

Why then is it such an easy road? Because you don't have to do anything to get on it. You are already traveling on it—you were born on it! How can you get off it? Turn in repentance to the narrow gate, trust Jesus Christ as your Savior. He said, *I am the Way, the Truth and the Life,* John 14.6. *I am the Door, by me if anyone enters in he (or she) shall be saved,* John 10.9.

We are all traveling onward, day by day, to eternity. Where are you going to spend eterntiy?

People are like fruit trees, 7.15-23

There are good trees and bad trees. How can we tell the difference? By the fruit, v.16. A good tree can't bear bad fruit, and a bad tree can't produce good fruit. It bears fruit according to its nature, vs.17,18. A thorn bush can only bear thorns not grapes. Whether it has only one thorn on it this year or a thousand it is still a thorn bush not a grapevine. A thistle can never produce figs. It must be a fig tree to bear figs.

15   Some bad people try to pretend they are good. The bad ones are like wolves trying to destroy the sheep-like people of the King. They try to imitate the sheep by putting sheepskins over themselves. Our Lord calls them false prophets. He warns us to be on our guard against them. How can we know them? By their fruits, that is by their lives, how they walk and talk. Only true believers can live like their King. Others may try to sound like Christians (vs. 21,22) but they have never truly received Christ into their hearts. So the King will expose them in the coming day of judgment, "I never knew you! Away

to destruction!" v.23. The bad tree will be cut down and thrown into hell fire, v.19.

Are you producing bad fruit: evil thoughts, bad words, wicked acts? Watch out for the coming judgment. Turn to the Lord and let Him save you from your sin. He will give you a new life and nature, 2 Corinthians 5.17. Then you will be able to bear the sweet fruits of right living through Jesus Christ, Philippians 1.11.

People are like builders, 7.24-27

Day by day we are all building our lives. The King tells us about two builders and two foundations. The builders are called Mr. Wise and Mr. Foolish. Their names come from the kind of foundation they built on.

A house is a place of refuge and shelter, a place to live in. Mr. Wise took great care to find a good solid rock for a foundation. Before he began to build upwards he looked downwards. He wanted a solid and lasting foundation under his home. After the house was built he moved into it and lived there. Then one day the stormy season began with violent winds and rain. It beat hard against that house and the river overflowed its banks and flooded the house. But the house stood firm—it did not fall because it had a good solid foundation—the ROCK.

Mr. Foolish had built his house too, by that time. But he had been in a hurry and didn't bother with any foundation. He just began to build right on the sand along the side of the stream. He may have built just as nice a house as Mr. Wise but he neglected the most important part—the Foundation. The same storm beat on his house and it fell apart with a great crash, killing Mr. Foolish and anybody else who was in the house. How sad! After all the work of building a home to go down with it into the floodwaters and be lost forever! All because it had no solid foundation.

Now the King used this simple illustration to help us understand what this Sermon on the Mount is all about. In verse 24 He tells us that Mr. Wise is a picture of people who listen to the King's words and then act on them, obey them. But Mr. Foolish also heard the King's words but did not obey them. He just went on his way and forgot what the King had said. One was saved and the other was lost. Mr. Foolish had traveled the wide, easy road; he bore bad fruit in his lifetime; he rejected the words of the King, so he ended up in the destruction and fire of hell.

But Mr. Wise had turned from the broad, easy road and entered the narrow gate in obedience to the King's words; he bore good fruit by the Holy Spirit; he put his whole trust in the King's words, so he escaped death and destruction, he entered into LIFE eternal. Which way are **you** traveling? On what are you building your life?

Many times in the Old Testament our Lord is called the ROCK. Look up Deuteronomy 32 and find four verses where it is mentioned. Also find a verse each in 2 Samuel 22, Psalm 28, 31, 61, 89. Write down the references in your Bible.

The King stresses the importance of His word. We should listen and obey Him. He is the only sure Foundation. Build your life on Him and on His Word, "these words of mine."

> On Christ the Solid Rock I stand
> All other ground is sinking sand.

The Reaction of the Crowd, 7.28,29

The crowd was surprised and amazed. They were so used to hearing their own scribes and teachers of the law. These were always quoting from the Law of Moses or from one of their great rabbis as their authority for what they were saying. But here was One who spoke on His own authority. In fact He had claimed that HIS word was of more authority than Moses himself! Fourteen times He said, "I say to you," or "I tell you the truth."

His authority is supreme. He **is** the King Himself and it was only right that they should bow to Him and obey Him. But we shall see that most were not willing to do this.

What is **your** response to His word?

Chapter 8

Miracles of the King

In chapters 5 to 7 the King has been speaking with authority. Now in chapters 8 and 9 He shows His **Power** in twelve wonderful miracles. This section has been called the Royal March of Miracles. The great King has power to **do**. He is the Great Physician. We will look at the first three cases in verses 1 to 16.

A Man with Leprosy, 8.1-4

In Bible times and lands many people suffered from various skin diseases. The worst was called leprosy. This dreadful disease was called the Creeping Death. It would eat away the flesh slowly as it covered more and more of the body. Fingers or toes, ears or nose would rot away and drop off. Lepers would lose feeling in parts of the body and could be standing on hot coals of fire without feeling pain in their feet. Leprosy was like a living death.

The Law of Moses stated that lepers should wear torn clothes and have their lower faces covered. They should shout out "Unclean, unclean," to warn other people of the danger of touching them. This was because the disease could easily be passed on to others. Lepers had to live away from other people, by themselves. (See Leviticus 13.45,46). This made life very hard and sad for them, and perhaps the saddest thing was that no doctor could cure them.

In this we can see a picture of ourselves as sinners in God's sight. We are unclean because of our sins, Psalm 51.1-6. Even our "good deeds" are filthy, Isaiah 64.6. Death is our sure end, and after that the judgment of God, Hebrews 9.27. How very sad all this is, how very hopeless — except . . . .

The leper in our chapter knew Someone who could help him. Isn't that exciting? During hundreds of years of history thousands of lepers had died in Israel without being healed, Luke 4.27. So how could the man in our story think he could be cured? As the large crowd came down out of the mountain he saw Jesus in the crowd. He rushed toward Him and knelt down at His feet, saying, "Lord I know You can make me clean—if only you are willing to!" How did he know that Jesus had power to cleanse his poor diseased body? No doubt he had seen Jesus make others well (as in chap. 4.23). So He could surely help him. But the problem was, would He be willing to? Nobody else cared for lepers. People didn't want to be near them for fear of "catching" the dread disease. Lepers were really outcasts from society.

But Jesus reached out His hand and **touched** him! What love! Did He care? Yes, He surely did. What a thrill to that poor leper. Perhaps he had been a leper for years. During all that time he had never felt a loving embrace. No one would even pat him on the shoulder in encouragement. But in love and sympathy Jesus actually touched him. "I am willing, be clean." Instantly every trace of leprosy disappeared. He was a new man — he was cured.

What can wash away **our** sin—leprosy? How can we be cleansed from all our sin? Here are several verses to look up and memorize: 1 John 1.7,8,9; Revelation 7.14.

What can wash away my sin?
Nothing but the blood of Jesus.

4 But why does the King order the man not to tell anyone about this wonderful miracle? Because there was something more important than just healing a body. Spiritual things are of first importance, physical things come second. The Law of Moses demanded sacrifice, see Leviticus 14.1-32. When a man was cleansed from leprosy he must go to the Jewish priest who examined him before declaring him ritually clean. The man must offer sacrifices to God. You will notice that the blood was shed in those sacrifices, vs. 6,7,14,25,28. This speaks of the precious blood of our Lord Jesus, 1 Peter 1.19. His greater sacrifice was going to be made on the Cross, chap. 27. That would do away with the Old Testament sacrifices, Hebrews 10.1-10. In the meantime the healed man must go directly to the priests to give testimony to **them** concerning this great Healer-King, Jesus.

(Those priests had never had to perform those rites before. We wonder if they had to look up Leviticus 14 to find out what to do? We wonder also if any of them believed in Christ, the true Messiah, as a result of this clear witness? They surely must have been amazed at it, to say the least. Consider Acts 6.7.)

So the great King revealed His POWER and His PURITY. He could touch the unclean one without becoming unclean Himself. No mere human being could do that. But He could and did because He was GOD.

The Roman Officer's Servant, 8.5-13

Now we read about a great man, vs.5,9, who had a great need or problem, v.6, but with great humility, v.8, and great faith, vs.6,10, he came to the great King (Lord, v.6), and received great results, v.13.

The officer is called a centurion because he commanded 100 soldiers in the Roman army. He was responsible to keep law and order in Capernaum. Often men in high position or rank become proud, Romans 1.30. But this officer was truly humble. This is the only way we can come to the Lord, see Psalm 138.6, James 4.6, 1 Peter 5.5.

6 He had a great problem. One of his servants became very sick, unable to move, and in great pain. What should he do? No doubt he could afford to call the best doctors in the province. But he did a wiser thing. He went (or sent) to Jesus with a simple, humble request for help. According to Luke 7 this officer had turned from his Roman idols toward the true living God of Judaism. Probably he knew about the healing of the nobleman's son elsewhere in Capernaum, John 4.46-54.

7 In verse 7 he stated his need to Jesus, who responded at once, "I will go and heal him." Jesus was not like human doctors who might say, "I will go and examine him to see if I can help him." No, Jesus calmly said He would go and HEAL him.

8 The officer's true humility shows clearly: I am not worthy, I don't deserve it. There are others in the Bible of whom the same is said. Look up these chapters and write down the verse and name or object:

Genesis 32. ____   _____

Matthew 3. ____   _____

Matthew 10. ____   _____

Matthew 22. ____   _____

Luke 15. ____   _____

Luke 15. ____   _____

Hebrews 11. ____   _____

Revelation 5. ____   _____

But there is One who IS worthy. Look up and fill in:

Revelation 4. ____   _____

Revelation 5. ____   _____

Now we hear the officer declaring his faith boldly, "All you need to do is just to **say the word** and my servant will be healed."

9 The officer explained why he had such faith. He himself had authority but he was under authority. He had to know how to

obey orders from his commanding officer before he could give orders to men under him. Here is a lovely picture of our Lord's position. He had come in obedience to His Father (sent by Him). And now HIS word of command must be obeyed. He could speak and the illness must be healed.

10-12 Such faith was rare in Israel. This officer was a Gentile, outside God's chosen people, Israel. They were rejecting their Messiah-King in unbelief, while by faith the outsiders, Gentiles, would be taking their places at the banquet-feast in heaven along with Abraham, Isaac and Jacob. Joy and blessing will be the sweet result of faith. Sorrow and pain result from unbelief. And forever.

13 The instant result of great faith in the great King was great healing. Go your way, your mission is finished. Your request has been granted. In full measure, just as you believed it would be. Completely healed that very hour—no repeat needed and no delay.

The word of the King brought the universe into being, Psalm 33.6. The word of the same King brought life and health to one of His creatures, v.13. His power meets our weakness.

Sicknesses at Peter's House, 8.14-16

Peter and Andrew lived in Capernaum where Jesus also lived for a time. Some think that perhaps He lived with Peter then (compare Mark 1.29,34). Peter's wife's mother was there too. She became very sick with a high fever. Most of us know how fever makes one very restless, thirsty and weak. But a touch of the King, v.14, and a word from the King, Luke 4.39, combined to drive the fever out of her body. Instant healing and power for service are seen. She arose and served the King at once, in His strength. That's the purpose of our salvation—to serve and glorify our King. His power overcomes our restlessness and weakness.

16 At evening it is nice to relax and rest after a busy day. But the crowds of sick and demon-possessed people kept coming to the house. So the King, still full of power, drove out each and every demon with His word of power. And **all** the sick were healed. The Great Physician never lost a case nor failed to bring full, complete healing. His power meets all our needs.

The Purpose of it all, 8.17

Now we have another "identity picture" from the Old Testament. All these miracles are to identify Jesus as the promised Deliverer-King. The prophet Isaiah had written (Isaiah 53.4), *He took our infirmities, weaknesses and illnesses and carried away our diseases.* Now Matthew tells us that this was fulfilled by Jesus at this time. No disease or illness could resist the power of the King.

Matthew 8.10-20

Isaiah 53 is the great prophecy concerning the sufferings of Messiah for **our sins**. Sickness and disease are the results of sin. During His life-ministry Christ took up the sicknesses of the people and healed them. But on the Cross He took up the **cause** of sickness—our sin. That is what the rest of Isaiah 53 refers to, see especially verse 5. *He was wounded, pierced, crushed, punished for our sins. By His wounds (on the cross) we are healed (spiritually from our sins)*, 1 Peter 2.24.

So the King, our Royal Healer, went about healing the bodies and minds of sick folk. It was all a picture of His work on the Cross when He suffered for our sins to heal us spiritually. So when we trust Him as our Savior we have forgiveness and peace. But can we not also expect complete physical healing now as a result of this great salvation? Some people think so. But that is future—we look forward to the redemption of the body at His coming again, see Romans 8.18-25. He surely can and does heal our bodily sicknesses now whenever it is in His will to do so. But often He does **not** because He has good purposes for His people's suffering now. Look up and carefully read these verses: Romans 8.18; 2 Corinthians 1.5-7; Philippians 3.10; Colossians 1.24; Hebrews 2.10; 1 Peter 2.20; 4.13; 4.16; 5.10; 1 Timothy 5.23; 2 Timothy 4.20.

A Warning, 8.18-22

18 The crowds were getting larger. The King was becoming "popular." In Matthew we notice the crowds mentioned 42 times (more than in Mark, Luke or John). Six times we read that He had pity on them and loved them: 9.36; 14.14; 15.30-32; 18.27,33; 20.34. So He fed them, chaps. 14 and 15; healed them, chaps. 14,15,17,19; and taught them, chaps. 13,15,23. His great love was interested in the need of each. Many responded to His love, and praised Him, 21.9; they respected Him as a Prophet, 21.46; they were amazed at Him, 22.33. And yet finally they rejected Him, 27.20-23! We do not read that many believed on Him. They were interested in earthly good things—healing, food, etc. He became popular. But our Lord did not come in order to be popular. He did not let the crowds get bigger and bigger. Instead five times we read that He left the crowds or sent them away. Find the verses in these chapters: 5,8,13,14,15. This was because He knew their hearts, many were not really trusting Him. They only wanted to make Him a king (to drive out the Romans), see John 6.15. But there must be a cross before there could be a crown.

19 It was then that a teacher of the law said he would follow Jesus wherever He went. Perhaps he was speaking the thoughts of others in the crowd.

20 In verse 20 Jesus gave a strong word of warning: It will be costly to follow Me! Following Jesus is not an easy, flower-covered

path. Jesus told him (and all of us) that His path is a hard one. Even the foxes have holes to sleep in and the birds have nests for their young ones. But there was no place on earth the Son of Man could call "home." A Homeless King! He was the Creator of the animals and birds and provided them with homes. Why was He, Himself, without a home? Because He had left His beautiful home in heaven. He was the rich One who became so very poor for us, read 2 Corinthians 8.9.

It is true He had lived in Joseph's and Mary's house for 30 years. But He could not stay there, He was not wanted by His family, John 7.3-5. He stayed with friends and disciples now and then, during His 3½ years of public service, Matthew 4.13; 9.10; 26.6. But read John 7.53-8.2. Stand beside Him as He watched all those people go to their own homes. No one invited Him to go with them. So walk along with Him as He treads the lonely path to the Mount of Olives. Watch Him as He sleeps under the stars, with perhaps a fox-hole nearby and a bird sitting on her nest in the olive tree above Him. This, no doubt, happened often, Luke 22.39. What a sight!

> *No room for the Baby in Bethlehem's inn —*
>   *Only a cattle shed;*
> *No place on this earth for the dear Son of God —*
>   *Nowhere to lay His head.*
> *Only a Cross did they give to our Lord —*
>   *Only a borrowed tomb;*
> *Today He is seeking a place in your heart —*
>   *Will you still say to Him NO ROOM?*

The Son of Man

20 Perhaps you noticed that in this verse is the first reference in Matthew to the title Son of Man. We find it 31 times in Matthew and it is an important title of the King. It is not simply saying that Jesus is a Man (son of a man). He is more than that. He is **the** Son of Man, meaning He is the Perfect Man, and more: He is GOD'S Perfect Man. And still more: He is the Perfect God-Man. He is called Son of God many times in the Bible, twelve times in Matthew. This tells of His Deity. As the Son of Man He is described in a twofold way: (1) in His humility and suffering on earth, and (2) in His coming glory and majesty.

Here are some of the references in Matthew where He is called the

Son of Man. Look up the verses in the following chapters. Write down the verse number and put in the description in the correct column. It will help you get a better understanding of this beautiful title of our King, the Son of Man.

Chapter	vs.	Ref. to Humiliation and Suffering	Ref. to Coming Glory
(examples)			
8.	20	deep poverty	
9.	6	came to forgive sins	
10.	23		coming again
11.	—		
12.	—		
	—		
	—		
13.	—		
16.	—		
	—		
17.	—		
	—		
19.	—		
24.	—		
	—		
	—		
25.	—		
26.	—		
	—		
	—		

21 Now another would-be follower asked the King to let him go back home to care for his father until he died and then he would follow Him. His father was not already dead or the man would have been home taking care of the funeral. But he used a common way of saying that he had responsibility of caring for his father. This of course is good. The Bible teaches that we are to love and honor our parents, Ephesians 6.1-3. We are to care for them if in need, 1 Timothy 5.8. So this was all right and proper UNTIL the King called. When HE says "Follow Me" what will a true disciple do? Obey at once, of course.

If our country calls a young man to war duty as a soldier he goes as ordered. He leaves parents and family, all his dear ones. He obeys the summons as a faithful citizen. Later on in Matthew 10.37-39 our King claims the total love and devotion of His followers. He tells us very plainly that love to HIM must come before love to anyone else. **HE must have first place**, 10.37. But this disciple in verse 21 said, *Let ME be first*. That is not the way a true disciple talks to his Master.

22 So the King gives the clear order, FOLLOW ME. If it means leaving homes or dear ones—so be it. If it means giving up a good job or houses or lands or whatever—so be it. HE has spoken—let us obey. But then the King added a strange sounding statement: *Let the dead bury their own dead*. What can He mean?

A dead person is one whose spirit has left the body. It is a corpse—without life. This is a picture of mankind's spiritual condition—no life toward God—dead in sinful disobedience. This is true of all unbelievers on earth, Ephesians 2.1-5. Such person are concerned only with this life on earth which is really a "living death." They have no love for the Lord Jesus or God. Let them do their natural thing—bury their dead. Luke adds, *But you go and preach the Kingdom of God*, Luke 9.60. That is the duty of all born again believers—don't live like the unsaved, but serve and obey your King. Preach HIS kingdom.

Yes, to follow the King will be a costly matter. We will learn more about this as we go on through Matthew.

The King of the Seas and a Fierce Storm, 8.23-27

23 After the brief delay of vs. 19-22, Jesus got into the boat. His disciples got in, pushed off and set sail for the other side of the lake. Jesus must have been weary because He was soon asleep. Had He spent all the previous night in prayer as He did in Luke 6.12?

24 But suddenly, without warning, a fierce storm hit the lake. This often happens in lakes surrounded by hills and mountains. Some of the disciples had been fishermen when Jesus called them to follow Him. (Can you remember at least four who were?) They were used to wind and rough seas. But this time it was different. The waves were

Matthew 8.22-28

covering the boat, it could easily sink, and they could all drown. Or—could they? Was it possible for that boat to sink and all aboard to drown? What do you think?

25 The disciples thought so. They saw the boat taking on more and more water. The wind was getting wilder and the waves higher. Deeply frightened they rushed to Jesus and woke Him. Save us, Lord, we are going to drown!

26 Then Jesus asked a remarkable question: Why are you so afraid? But didn't they have good reason to be afraid? Weren't they sinking to their watery graves? He answered His own question: How little your faith is! Do you see the problem they had? Fear came from lack of faith. They had forgotten the Lord's word, *Let's go over to the other side*, Mark 4.35. They forgot who He was and what He had said. No storm or enemy, not even Satan himself, could stop their safe arrival! Here was the King-Ruler of all nature, standing up and rebuking the wind and waves, *Peace! Be quiet! be still!*, Mark 4.39. Instantly the wind stopped blowing and waves became perfectly calm.

27 The disciples were amazed. Aren't you? Who is this One? The wonderful Creator of the winds and seas, Genesis 1. The Controller of the universe, Colossians 1.15-17, Psalm 107.29, Job 38.11. And of you?

Our lives are like a voyage on a great sea. There are many storms we must face. Dangers and problems can be too great for us to safely pass through. But if we have Christ in our lives (our little boats) we can "smile at the storm." Why? He has promised to be with His own and to take them safely to home-port, heaven, Hebrews 13.5,6; John 10.27-30. Let's not doubt Him when the storms come, but let's trust Him and not be afraid, Psalm 56.3,11. *Call to me in your day of trouble, I'll deliver you*, Psalm 50.15. His answer will be PEACE.

> *The winds and the waves shall obey my will:*
> *Peace, be still.*
> *Whether the anger of storm-tossed sea*
> *Or demons or men or whatever it be*
> *No water can swallow the boat where lies*
> *The Master of ocean and earth and skies!*
> *They all shall sweetly obey MY will—*
> *Peace, Peace, be still.*

Power Over Demons, 8.28-34

28 So they arrived safely at the other shore. This territory was Gadara. (Some old Bibles called it Gergesa or Gerasa). It was at the south part of the Sea of Galilee. There are still many old tombs among the rocks in that area.

Living among the tombs were two men, possessed by demons. Some old Bibles call them devils, but there is only one devil, Satan, chapter 4.1-10. He is the ruler of the kingdom of darkness. Who then are these demons? In Matthew 25.41 our Lord refers to Satan and his angels. These demons are fallen angels who serve Satan. They are called evil or unclean spirits, Mark 1.23; Luke 4.33. As they serve Satan they have at least two motives: (1) to further his work and authority among human beings; and (2) to hinder God's purposes for mankind.

From New Testament references to demons we learn some important facts about them. They are very powerful, even violent, v. 28; Luke 8.29. They are spirit beings but want bodies to live in so they can do their evil deeds, chap. 8.31; Luke 11.24-26. They can cause bodily harm, Mark 9.18, blindness, Matthew 12.22, suffering and diseases, Luke 13.11-17, muteness, Matthew 9.32,33. There are different kinds of demons, Matthew 17.21. Sometimes they cause bodily sickness and sometimes mental illness, Mark 9.18. When they enter a person they take charge of him or her. They rule over the will and yet they are separate from the person. There seems to be a double consciousness. The demon can be spoken to and it can speak (through the person's voice) and yet the person can speak and understand things also.

There are many demons. Mark 5.13 tells of at least 2,000 in just this story. They are too powerful for human beings to overcome them, v.28. But all demons are subject to our Lord Jesus Christ. It is very important to notice that they knew and confessed who Jesus is—the Son of God, v.29. He is King.

—They knew their judgment is coming, v.29. They are doomed.
—they could only humbly beg Him, v.30; they dare not demand.
—they must obey Him and always do, v.32. He is supreme.
—they tremble in fear of God, James 2.19. They know He exists.
—they fear torture and punishment, v.29. There is no escape for them.

Here are some ways they are described in the New Testament:

        Evil spirit, Mark 9.25, Luke 4.33
        Crippling spirit, Luke 13.11
        Wicked spirit, Luke 11.26
        Lying, deceiving spirit, 1 Timothy 4.1
        Unclean spirit, Luke 4.36; 6.18
        Deaf and mute spirit, Mark 9.25
        Spirit of fortune-telling, Acts 16.16
        Spirit of falsehood, error, 1 John 4.1-6
        Foul, evil spirit, Revelation 18.2.

How sad it is that such cruel, evil spirits can enter and live in human beings! They possessed the two men in this story, and many others in the four Gospels. The persons involved were under their strong control and could not escape. But the Good News of Jesus Christ is this: HE can set the captive free, 2 Timothy 2.26; Hebrews 2.14,15.

29 These two demon-possessed men must have seen Jesus coming in the distance. They called out loudly to Him. But note it was the demons who were calling out, What do you want with **us** to torture us before the right, appointed time? They knew they were wrongfully living in these two suffering men. They knew they were going to be punished on the judgment day. They knew exactly who Jesus was—they confessed He was the Son of God. They knew HE was the One who was going to judge them. Eternal fire is prepared for the Devil **and** his angels, Matthew 25.41. They knew their judgment would be torture and that they deserved it.

30,31 They also knew Jesus was about to drive them out of these two men. They knew they would have to obey His word. They begged Jesus not to send them into the deep, bottomless pit, Luke 8.31, where they could have been sent, see 2 Peter 2.4, Jude 6, Revelation 9.1,2,11; 11.7; 17.8; 20.1,3. They begged for a 'stay of execution," that is, a delay in punishment. They begged to be allowed to enter the large herd of pigs feeding on the hillside near the lake. The Lord Jesus didn't have to grant their request. His power over them was complete, and He has no mercy for evil spirits.

32 But He spoke one word of command: GO. Instantly they all came out of the two men and entered those pigs, all 2,000 of them, Mark 5.13. What power this King has! One word can stop a violent storm and bring perfect calm on the sea, v.26. And one word can deliver two men of 2,000 violent demons and bring perfect peace in the heart, Mark 5.15.

33 The whole herd of pigs tumbled down the steep bank into the sea and drowned. The herd-keepers were, of course, helpless to stop them. All they could do was to run to town and report the matter to their employers. They also reported what had happened to the two men. The whole town heard about it all. What was their response? What is yours?

There are so many who say, What a loss! (In today's market it could amount to hundreds of thousands of dollars). How unfair that those farmer-hog producers should suffer such a loss. They weren't to blame for the demons.

But there are others who say, What a blessing—two suffering, miserable men were freed, saved, rescued. How wonderful to see them delivered and restored to their homes and families.

Which way do you look at this miracle? Your answer will tell you what the King thinks of your attitude. Look up Mark 8.36,37. Do you see how our Lord values one soul? Worth more than the whole world—valuable pigs and all! Here two souls were rescued from Satan's grip. That's worth more than two worlds! Those two souls were worth enough to our blessed Lord to cause Him to give His life as a ransom-price on their behalf on the Cross of Calvary. See 1 Peter 1.18,19. So the arithmetic of heaven is very clear about what true values are.

But there is still a moral problem some may have.

Our Lord is King over all. He came to earth to bless not to curse; to heal not to wound. This act seems to be an unkind act. Why did He not send the evil spirits directly to their doom? Why did He allow them first to enter the pigs and then to their doom?

Perhaps we have a clue in the fact the animals were pigs and not sheep or cows. The Old Testament gave the Jews some very clear rules about what they could and could not eat. Look up Leviticus 11.7 and Deuteronomy 14.8. The Jews were not allowed to eat pork nor even to touch the carcasses of pigs! And Isaiah 66.17 tells of God's hatred of such things. What then were the Jews in the region of Gadara doing with so many pigs around? We realize there were many Gentiles living around those parts then, but the religion of the area was still Judaism. If Jews owned the pigs they were breaking the law of Moses. If Gentiles were the owners they at least were insulting the Jew's religion and defiling the land.

We suppose this loss may have put the owners "out of business." But the Lord Jesus also put other evil men out of business, as in the temple, John 2.13-16. Also see Acts 16.19.

So we agree with the comments of one Bible teacher. He said that the Lord performed two acts of blessing here: (1) blessing on two men rescuing them from the terrible power of Satan, and (2) blessing on the community in delivering it from the defilement of pigs.

34 Now what was the response of the whole town? Did they praise God for such a mighty act of deliverance—two men freed from 2,000 demons? Not at all! Contrast ch. 9.8 and Luke 5.26. Did they beg for forgiveness or mercy for having the pigs around at all? No. Did they dare to ask for repayment of the loss of the pork? No again. Their guilty consciences would not allow them to do that. What did they do? They begged HIM to leave their region! And Jesus **did** just as they requested, 9.1. And that is the saddest part of the whole story. We never read that He ever returned to their region again. Compare Exodus 10.28,29 and Matthew 23.37,38.

....

Note on verse 29: SON OF GOD. This is a remarkable testimony to

Matthew 8.34

the Deity of Christ — Demons confessed it. Matthew gives a number of other testimonies to His deity. Find the verses and fill in names.

(Example) Matthew 1 v. _23___ Who: prophet Isaiah_____
Matthew 3 v. _____ _____
Matthew 4 vs. _&_ _____
Matthew 14 v. _____ _____
Matthew 16 v. _____ _____
Matthew 26 v. _____ _____
Matthew 27 v. _____ _____
Matthew 27 v. _____ _____

Chapter 9

Miracles of the King (cont'd)

This chapter continues the Royal March of Miracles. The great power of the King is shown in five individual healings and one general group, v.35. In each we see pictures of sinners in their need of spiritual healing.

Power to Forgive and Heal, 9.1-8

1 No doubt with heavy heart Jesus got into the boat on the Gadara coast. His love had been rejected, so He crossed the lake back to Capernaum.

2 There was a paralyzed man in town, lying helpless on his bed-mat.
Some friends wanted to help him, so they carried him on his bed-mat to the house where Jesus was teaching a crowd of people. Mark and Luke tell us the house was so packed with people the men couldn't enter. So they climbed up the outside stairway to the flat roof. They made an opening in the roof and let the man down right in front of Jesus. They believed the King could and would heal their friend.

Jesus saw their faith. How? He sees right inside everyone's heart. He knows if we are really trusting Him. In this case they didn't even have to ask the Lord to heal him. The King knew the man's needs. Others thought the man's first need was a healed body. But Jesus saw his deeper need: to have his sins taken away. He put first things first and said, Cheer up, son; your sins are forgiven! What joy filled the man's heart! Sins all forgiven—what a precious gift. Do you have it?

3 Some teachers of the law had come from Jerusalem to check on this new Teacher, Luke 5.17. When they hear this word they were startled, and thought to themselves, That is blasphemy. He is speaking against God. Only God can forgive sins. (But the reason Jesus can and does forgive sins is that He IS God, ch. 8.29.)

4 The King knew what they were thinking, see Psalm 94.11; 139.2.
He is all-knowing so no one can hide even one thought from Him. He reads our thoughts like an open book.

5 So He asked them an important question. Which is easier, to say, Your sins are forgiven, or to say, Get up and walk? Of course they were thinking it was easy to **say**, You are forgiven, because that's inside the heart, who could ever disprove it? But what do you say? Which was easier for Jesus, to heal a body or heal a soul? For Jesus to

heal the body He only had to speak the word of power. But to forgive sins He had to lay down His life on the Cross. It cost Him His life!

6 But those law-teachers didn't answer the King. They couldn't because neither was possible for them. But what is impossible with men is possible with God. And Jesus is God. So He said, *Get up, take up your bed-mat and go home!*

7 The man did just that. Paralyzed one minute, full of health and strength the next. How wonderful!

8 The crowd was filled with fear and awe and they praised God.
Nothing is said about the law-teachers. They sat in stubborn, cold silence of unbelief. Power **on earth** to forgive sins. If we are not forgiven while here on earth we can never be forgiven in the next world!

Power to Attract, 9.9-13

9 Jesus walked away from the house, going along the lake front.
There was a tax-collector's booth where the government agent collected tax on the fish or produce passing through the port. Even at that distant date the people didn't like to pay taxes, especially to the foreign power that ruled over them—Rome. The Jews hated any other Jew who took a government job like collecting the taxes for Rome. Public servants like that were called Publicans; they were always classed along with sinners, like immoral persons, criminals, etc. The Pharisees considered them all as outcasts from decent society. See chapter 11.19; 18.17; 21.31.

But Jesus saw the **man** inside the booth, not what people thought about the booth and position. Others might despise him but Jesus did not (see chap. 12.20). He called to the despised Matthew: Follow Me! At once Matthew obeyed. He got up, left everything, Luke 5.28, and followed his new King.

> *I heard HIS call, Come follow,*
>   *That was all.*
> *My gold grew dim*
> *My soul went after HIM.*
> *Who would not follow when they heard HIM call?*
>   (Selected)

Have **you** done so?

10 Luke tells us that Matthew spread a great feast for his new Lord and King, chap. 5. But here Matthew only modestly records the Lord was sitting at dinner in the house. He must have invited all his fellow tax-collectors to the feast, also the "sinners" of town. Jesus and His disciples were there also. Perhaps Matthew wanted to have a

"farewell dinner" for his old companions, so he took the opportunity to introduce them to his new Master and King, Jesus. What a nice way to witness for his Lord!

11 Of course the Pharisees would hear about this. Or they may have seen it as they passed by Matthew's home. They just could not hold back their scorn and disgust. When they had opportunity they asked some of Jesus' disciples why their master ate with such people.

12-14 Of course Jesus knew about their question, as in verse 4. His answer is beautiful as He makes two clear statements: (1) It is only sick people who need a doctor. Only when we feel sick do we go to the doctor. Sin is a disease which needs healing. (2) It is only sinners who need a Savior. Only when we are in danger will we call for rescue. Here is a simple but important saying to remember:

Only Jesus saves sinners,
and Jesus saves only sinners.

He did not come to save good people, there are none—Romans 3.10-12. Some people **think** they are good enough for heaven but they are mistaken. Have you admitted you are a sinner? If you have there is hope for you!

But between the two statements the King challenged those teachers of the law to look back into their Old Testament and learn what Hosea 6.6 means, *I want mercy and kindness, not sacrifices of animals.* In other words, Go and learn what God's heart is like. Is God pleased with many sacrifices brought by people with unrepentant hearts? Not at all. The reader should read Isaiah 1.11-18. Micah 6.7,8. God is the God of Mercy but He can show mercy only to **guilty** people. Jesus came to call sinners to repent, Luke 5.32. Read Luke 15, note especially verses 2,7,10,18,32.

Perhaps the reader is wondering why Mark and Luke refer to Levi instead of Matthew. Some Bible teachers think Levi was his family name which he dropped when he became a disciple of our Lord. Others think Jesus named him Matthew at the time of his conversion (as He changed Simon's name to Peter). But the Bible doesn't say, so we can't be sure. We know only that Levi and Matthew are the same person.

Power to Satisfy, 9.14-17

14 We find some followers of John the Baptizer coming to Jesus. John had been put in prison, chapter 4.12. His disciples had remained true to him and lived the way he had taught them. They often fasted and went without food for certain times. The Pharisees also did this as a religious duty. But they noticed that the disciples of Jesus did not fast. They asked Him why not?

15 Fasting is a sign of sorrow. Jesus told John's disciples that while He was with His followers they were not full of sorrow. He was the Bridegroom and they were like guests at a marriage feast. Weddings are times of great joy, singing and gladness. What made the disciples of Jesus joyful? Their King was with them. His joy was their portion, John 15.11. So why should they fast and be sad? The time would come when He would be taken away from them (chaps. 26 & 27). Then they were sorrowful and "fasted" in their hearts at least. But He arose from the dead and His word to them was REJOICE, 28.9. Now He is alive and has promised to be with His followers always, 28.20. He will never leave nor forsake us, Hebrews 13.5. So we are to rejoice at all times, 1 Thessalonians 5.16.

16 Then the King used two illustrations to explain what He meant.

The first was about patching an old garment. It was worn out, so why waste time trying to patch it? If you sew a new piece of cloth on the old garment it will shrink and tear. (Luke adds that the piece of new cloth was taken from a new garment so the new garment was spoiled also.)

17 Neither do people put new wine into old, dried wineskins. The old ones will burst, they cannot hold new wine. What the King is saying to John's disciples (and to us) is this: I give my followers NEW life, joy and peace. This cannot be squeezed into the old lifestyle. There is a new beginning, they are a new creation in Christ, 2 Corinthians 5.17. The old garments and wineskins of Old Testament lawkeeping are done away in Christ. New joy fills our hearts and lives.

Power to Heal, 9.20-22

In verses 18 and 19 Jesus was on His way to the home of the ruler of the synagogue. Large crowds pressed around Him, Mark 5.24. Among them was a thin, pale woman who was sick. No doctor had been able to stop her bleeding and she was getting worse. She knew Jesus could heal her, so she worked her way through the crowd and reached out and touched His garment. At once her bleeding stopped and she was healed. Perhaps she wanted to keep it secret because of shame. According to Old Testament law she had been "unclean" and was not allowed to enter the Lord's presence in the temple, see Leviticus 15.26.

Luke 8 tells us she touched the edge or border of His coat. In the Old Testament the people of God were told to wear a border on their outer garment with blue ribbon or tassels. This was to remind Israelites that they belonged to the Lord and should obey His law, Numbers 15.37-40, Deuteronomy 22.12. This suggests a lovely witness to our

Lord Jesus. His blue ribbon or tassels would be a reminder that He had come from heaven, sent by His Father, to seek and save the lost.

Jesus knew at once that she had touched Him and was healed. He drew from her a confession of what had happened and told her that her faith was rewarded. It put her in personal touch with Him. If I touch **Him** I will be healed. And she was. Have you?

Notice how tenderly the King spoke to this new believer: Daughter! The unclean one was made clean. She is now a member of God's family, accepted instead of rejected. Instead of sadness and discouragement she hears the words, Be of good cheer. How loving and kind is our great King. Praise His Name!

Power over Death, 9.18,19,23-26

18,19 The ruler of the synagogue was named Jairus, Mark 5, Luke 8.

He came to Jesus and humbly knelt before Him. His heart was heavy because his twelve year old daughter was dying. He, too, knew that Jesus could make her well. So he asked Jesus to come and put His hand on her, "and she **will** live." What faith, humble but confident!

So Jesus got up right away and went with the sorrowing father. The disciples went along, as did the large crowd as we have seen.

23 When they arrived at Jairus' house they found a noisy crowd, no doubt wailing the death wail. The flute players had arrived also, playing the sad music of death. Everyone was expecting to go with the family to the cemetery. No one paid any attention to Jesus when He arrived.

24 But the King took charge at once. He told all the noisemakers to go away. Wailing and sad music were not necessary or wanted. Jesus said, *Go away; the girl is not dead but asleep.* But they knew that she had died, Luke 8.53, and they laughed and mocked Jesus.

25 But Jesus drove them all out of the house. Why? They did not believe in Him, compare chapter 13.58. Blessing only comes to Faith. But why did Jesus say the girl was asleep and not dead? A dead person is beyond the reach of human beings. Jairus could not call his darling daughter back. She had died to him and to all the family. But she was not beyond the reach of the King! He was able to call her back to life exactly as we would call and awaken a sleeping person. That's just what He did. He took her by the hand and she got up. The great King has power over death.

26 No wonder this news spread all through that region. Here was One who is the Conqueror of Death. Matthew is saying to us all: Behold, take a good look at, the great KING.

Matthew 9.18-36 63

More Power to Heal, 9.27-34

I. Two blind men, vs. 27-31.

27 "Have mercy on us, Son of David." The speakers were two blind men who needed mercy. They cried to the right Person. Note they addressed Him as Son of David. In chapter 20.30,31 we read about two other blind men who also called Him Son of David. This seems to be a title of the Messiah, the Promised Deliverer, which specially relates Him to Israel. The prophet Isaiah, chapter 35.5, told how the blind would be given sight when the King came. (Read the whole chapter.) The nation of Israel was blind to this wonderful Deliverer and rejected Him; see Isaiah 53 and Romans 11.30.

28 In the house the blind men came to Jesus and He asked them if they believed He could do this. They replied, Yes, Lord.

29,30 He touched their eyes, saying, According to your FAITH it will be done. They were healed. But He sternly told them not to tell anyone. Why did He say that? We believe this and other similar references tell us something important. The King was not seeking mere popularity nor acting to satisfy mere curiosity. He never did miracles just to entertain people. He was looking for FAITH.

II. The Demon-possessed Mute, vs. 32-34.

32 As the healed blind men left somebody brought a demon-possessed man who could not talk. Jesus cast out the demon and the man was able to speak. Once again the Power of the King is seen. Power over demons.

33 The crowd which was present this time had not seen Jesus cast out demons before, so they were amazed and exclaimed that they had never seen anything like this.

34 But again the proud Pharisees refused to be amazed. They refused to believe in the Lord Jesus. Instead they tried to "explain away" this miracle. They said that Jesus drove out demons by means of the prince of demons. In other words they said Jesus was a servant of Satan! What a terrible thing to say! We will see how the King deals with this in the next chapter and in chapter 12.

The Needy Harvest Field, 9.35-38

35 Jesus now went on another "missionary trip" through all the towns and villages of Galilee. He **taught** in the synagogues, He **preached** the Good News, and He **healed** every kind of sickness.

36 As He saw the many needy people His great heart loved them. He saw them as sheep without a shepherd, multitudes in need, helpless, restless and defenceless, and He longed to bless them. See Numbers 27.17.

37 He turned to His disciples and told them that the harvest is plentiful but there are not enough laborers to bring it in.

38 Then He told them what to do: PRAY. Pray to the Lord of the Harvest to send out workers. The field is the world, chapter 13.38. The harvest represents lost men and women and children—all souls for whom Christ died. The Lord of the Harvest is the Lord Himself who through the Holy Spirit directs the work of harvesting today. The task is great: preach the Good News to every person in the world. That was the parting order of our risen King, Matthew 28 and Mark 16. Do you realize how many people that means? Today there are more than four thousand million persons on earth, and MOST of them have never clearly heard our King's message of Good News.

Are we praying earnestly to the Lord to send out workers?
Are we each one willing to pray, Here am I, Lord, send **me***?*
(Isaiah 6.8.)

....

Our blessed Lord and King has shown us in chapters 8 and 9 how very powerful He is. He has power to forgive the sinner, to attract the unwanted and worthless, to satisfy the heart, to raise to life the lifeless, to heal the helpless, the hopeless, the sightless and the speechless. Power to meet every kind of need in our lives. What a powerful and glorious King! Praise His Name!

Chapter 10

Twelve Apostles Sent Out

1   Jesus called the twelve disciples to Him. He gave them authority or power to drive out evil spirits and heal all kinds of diseases, as He Himself had been doing. He gave them this power so that other people could see that they were true representatives of the King.

2-4   Matthew here lists the names of the twelve disciples. For the differences with the other Gospels, see Appendix I.

5   In chapter 9.38 the disciples were told to pray that workers would be sent out into the harvest fields. Now the King sends **them** as the workers. They are now Apostles, which means sent ones, or missionaries. Apostles are direct representatives, ambassadors of the King. They speak for the King and act on HIS authority and behalf.

Then He gave them their instructions which we find in the rest of this chapter. But we should notice there are three distinct sections, each ending with, "I tell you the truth," vs. 15, 23 and 42. The instructions in Mark 6 and Luke 9 end at verse 15 in our chapter. The first section, vs. 5-15, applied to the local, immediate mission just before them. This ended at the death and resurrection of the King. Then section 2, vs. 16-23, covers the period of time from the Acts through the Epistles, probably ending with the judgment of Israel, the destruction of Jerusalem in A.D. 70. The third section covers general instructions and principles for all this present age.

Section 1 - 10.5-15

5,6   This mission was very limited in location. They were not to go to any Gentiles or Samaritans. These lived between Judea and Galilee. They were descendants of heathen Gentiles who were moved into Samaria by the foreign king of Assyria. See 2 Kings 17.24-29.

These had married with some of the Jews who had been left in the land. They were hated by the Jews. Some Jews would not even eat from dishes used by a Samaritan. See John 4.9.

The Good News must first go to the lost sheep of Israel. The apostles were to have pity on the lost sheep, like their Master did, chapters 15.24; 9.36. Israel as a nation was lost and needed the Good Shepherd. Read Jeremiah 50.6,17; Ezekiel 34.2-6. Also Isaiah 53.6 refers to individuals in Israel. So the King was sending His ambassadors first to His own people, Israel, before reaching out to the Gentiles. See Romans 1.16.

7,8 Here is the purpose of their mission: (1) the **message** to be preached: the Kingdom of heaven is near; (2) the **miracles** would give proof they truly represented the King; they would do just as He had been doing in chapters 8 and 9: (3) the **manner** of serving— freely, without charge. They were not to collect any fees for their services as doctors do. Instead they were to give and help freely. Look up Deuteronomy 15.11. See also Acts 8.18-24; and 20.35.

9 So they were not to collect pay for their services. Neither should they take money along to pay for living expenses.

10 Neither were they allowed to take along extra clothes nor a "beggar's bag" for food. The worker is worthy of his keep.

11-14 Here is the plan of action: (1) They should look for someone willing to welcome them into his home. They were the King's messengers with His message to His subjects. All Israelites should have welcomed them, but they didn't, John 1.11: (2) Greet people with the common Hebrew greeting, Peace, which included the idea of well-being and prosperity; (3) Stay at that home until they left the town; (4) They should "take back" the greeting if the people refused to receive them; (5) They should shake the dust off their feet when leaving that house or town. This was a sign that they did not share even a small bit of their guilt of rejecting the King and His messengers. See illustrations of this in Acts 13.51; 18.6. (The Jews had a custom of shaking dust from their feet whenever they returned to Judea from a Gentile country.)

15 This is a very sad verse. The King sternly warns that rejection brings judgment. There **is** going to be a day of judgment. Sodom and Gomorrah were two very wicked cities that God had to destroy because of their sin. See Genesis 18 and 19. The people of those cities will be at that judgment. So will the people from the towns which rejected the King. But the harder punishment will be on those who had greater opportunity, the privilege of hearing God's Good News of salvation. Read carefully Romans 1.18-2.29 which explains how God will judge various kinds of people.

Section 2 - 10.16-23

Now the King speaks about a new phase of their mission. They are going to suffer persecution. This did not happen to them before the Cross. The Lord protected them, as in John 18.8,9. But after He went back to heaven we read much in the book of Acts about the persecution they received.

16 Verse 16 doesn't sound like a victory march! The King wasn't sending His servants to fight to victory, John 18.36. Instead they would be like sheep amid a pack of savage wolves, weak and defenseless. So they should be cautious and wise, like snakes, and harmless and gentle like doves. Sheep are very needy animals, they need a good shepherd. So the King is telling them to keep close to Himself, the Good Shepherd. They would need wisdom, and the fear of the Lord is the beginning of wisdom, Proverbs 9.10. Their outward way of life was to be gentle and innocent, pleasing to the Lord. We have already seen the dove is a picture of the Holy Spirit, chapter 3.16. They would need His guidance and help.

17 So He warns them to be on guard against men, especially **religious** men! They would arrest and beat the King's servants! See how this took place in Acts 22.19; 26.11, also Acts 17.

18 For the Lord's sake they would be arrested and tried before governors and kings of the **Gentiles**. So we see how this time is different from that of verse 5. Read Acts 24-26 and 2 Timothy 4.16,17. Notice some other differences: (1) After the Lord's death and resurrection they went to the whole world which included Gentiles, Matthew 28.19,20; Mark 16.15; Acts 13.46. (2) The message is not primarily preaching the kingdom of heaven but the good news of salvation through faith in Christ, as in the Acts and Epistles; (3) The temporary, passing gifts of miracles were being phased out; emphasis is on faith and forgiveness. (4) In Acts 18.3, 2 Thessalonians 3.7-10 and elsewhere, the Apostles worked with their hands to pay expenses. Elsewhere they received gifts from other believers, as Romans 15.27. This contrasts with verse 10 of our chapter.

19,20 Now they would be arrested and tried but they could trust the Holy Spirit to give the right words of defense. Compare Acts 4.8-13. In John 14 and 15 the Holy Spirit is called the Helper and Counselor. He stands by our side when we need strength, Acts 7.54-60.

21 The King speaks about even harder trial: family hatred. Brothers and sisters would turn into enemies. Parents would be put to death for their faith. Many years ago one believer was arrested and was going to be put to death. His accusers said to him, "Don't you know that the whole world is against you?" (Meaning, you don't have a chance!) But the Christian replied, "Well then, I'm against the whole world!" That's the brave faith the King's followers can have. He tells them to stand firm until the end and they would surely be delivered. They should not give in. Even though they die they would be the winners—a crown of life is theirs, Revelation 2.10. See notes on chapter 24.13.

23 The King tells them to flee to another city if possible. See examples in Acts 17.5-10; 2 Corinthians 11.32,33. This is not because they were cowards but to spread the Good News to other places as well.

Here we find the second statement, "I tell you the truth." The first ended the first mission at the Cross. This one closes the King's dealings with Israel, perhaps at the destruction of Jerusalem in A.D. 70. Israel will be taken up again after the Church has gone to heaven at the Rapture. The message of the Kingdom of heaven will be preached again just before the King comes in power and great glory. We will learn more about this in chapters 24 and 25.

Section 3 - 10.24-42, *General Instructions*

24,25 We find our Lord using three titles for Himself as relating to His followers: Teacher and Disciples (to learn from Him); Master and Bondslaves (to serve Him); Head of family and Members of family (to obey Him). In all three relationships we are to be **like** our Lord in each case. We can expect the same treatment He received. We will be misunderstood and they will say bad things about us.

But what does it mean when He was called Beelzebub? In chapter 9:34 His enemies claimed He cast out demons by the "prince of demons." In 2 Kings 1.1,2 Baalzebub was called the god of Ekron. There the Philistines worshiped it, and linked it with sickness. King Ahaziah tried to consult this idol regarding his accident and God punished him for that. Later on the Jews linked all disease with evil spirits and evidently chose the name of this idol to represent the chief of all evil spirits. It was the worst name they could call Jesus.

26,27 The King tells His followers to expect to have bad and untrue things said about them; they should not be afraid. They (and we) are to: (1) Hear His Word in private (as we study, meditate and pray He speaks to us); then (2) Preach it in public, witnessing to those around us by our life and lips.

28 Again He says, Don't be afraid of men. The most they can do is kill the body. They cannot touch the real person, the "I" who lives inside, called here the Soul. See Luke 12.19,20.

But there is One to be feared and it is not Satan. Satan has no power to throw anyone into hell. Satan himself will **be** thrown there. Revelation 20.10. By whom? By God, the Creator of all life and the great Judge of **all**. We should fear HIM. See Revelation 20.11-15.

29-31 But verses 29 to 31 tell us about His loving care for His own.

The sparrow is the most common bird to most people. In Bible times they were so common they sold two for one small coin. If a person bought four the seller would throw in a fifth one free, five for two coins, Luke 12.6. There are something like a thousand million birds in the world. We do not know how many are sparrows, but God knows each one that falls to the ground and dies. One Bible teacher says, "God attends the funeral of every sparrow that dies!" He cares for the lowly sparrow. How very much more does He care for His own children, believers in Christ. He even knows the number of the hairs on their heads. He puts special value on even the little things in our lives. Look at Luke 21.18; Acts 27.34. So don't be afraid,

His eye is on the sparrow
And I know He cares for me.

32,33 Now the King calls for brave confession by His followers. If they have such a loving Father and they fear Him only, they will boldly confess Him before men. This includes a steady, godly walk backing up the words of the lips. To such the King says that He will acknowledge them before all heavenly beings.

To deny Him means to declare we do not know Him nor have anything to do with Him. See chapter 26.69-75. The King will have to disown such before His Father. This does not mean that a Christian can be lost if he denies Christ like Peter did. Peter was not lost—he was rebuked and restored, John 21.15-19. But it refers to unbelievers, like Judas, who turn from Christ entirely and disown Him finally. See 2 Timothy 2.11-13.

34 The King says something which may sound strange to us. Did He really mean He did not come to bring Peace? Didn't the angels sing "peace on earth" when He was born? But here He says He came to bring a sword not peace. What can He mean? We suggest first of all that the key to this verse is the word "bring." He did not come to bring peace, but to **make** peace by His blood shed on the Cross, Ephesians 2.15,16; Colossians 1.20. Peace cannot co-exist with sin. Our sins separated us from a holy God, Isaiah 59.2, hence no peace, verse 8. So Christ came to make peace. That is where the sword comes in.

The sword is an instrument of death. Zechariah 13.7 foretells His death as being like God striking His Son (Shepherd) with the sword of judgment. Also when Jesus was born His mother, Mary, was warned that a sword would pierce her own soul. This spoke of His death. So we suggest He must be sacrificed as our Peace Offering (Leviticus 3.1, etc.) before He could rightly be called our Prince of Peace, Isaiah 9.6. In this way we see the first meaning of this verse refers to our Lord's work of redemption on the cross.

35,36 Here we find the second meaning. The results of confessing Christ before men would be like a sword in the lives and families of His true followers. Here He quotes from Micah 7.6 as another "identity key" or picture of His Kingship. To follow this King would be painful. Even today in many parts of the world it is very costly to confess Christ. Many have lost their homes, their jobs and even their lives.

Really this was the experience of our Lord Himself, so His followers can expect the same. John 7.5; 15.18-21; Psalm 41.9; 55.12-14.

37-39 Important choices are given in these verses. Believers are commanded to love and honor their parents, Ephesians 6.1-3. They are to love and care for their children, Ephesians 6.4. But they are to love Christ above all others. He demands total loyalty to Himself, taking up the cross. The cross is another instrument of death. Verse 39 means (1) taking our place as a condemned criminal and marching off to our death. Not bodily death necessarily, but putting to death the old self-life. It means the end of self-pleasing, self-direction, self-rule; let HIM be King of our lives. Carefully read Romans 6. We must choose between the lower life and the higher, the natural and the spiritual, the temporal and the eternal. (2) Included also may be physical life laid down in martyrdom. Many, many believers have lost their lives in this way. But the promise is true: shall find it, in resurrection, Revelation 2.10.

Jim Elliot was a young missionary to the Auca Indians in Ecuador. He and four others were savagely killed as they tried to reach these Indians with the Good News of God's salvation. But before Jim ever went to Ecuador he wrote these important words:

He is no fool who gives what he cannot keep in order to gain what he cannot lose.

Think about this. The King has said that whoever holds onto his life for himself will surely lose it. But "whoever loses his life for MY sake shall find it." For whom are YOU living? For self or Christ?

40 Jesus clearly shows His Oneness with His Father. He who receives Me receives the One who sent Me (the Father). John's gospel gives

Matthew 10.35-42

many more references to this Oneness, and to the Deity of Christ. What we do to the one we do to the other. Look up these references and write in the verse:

(Example)   Receive —   Matthew 10 v. __40__
           Honor —   John 5 v. _____
           Know —   John 8 v. _____
           Believe —   John 12 v. _____
           Trust —   John 14 v. _____
           See —   John 14 v. _____
           Come to — John 14 v. _____
           Love —   John 14 v. _____
           Ask —   John 16 v. _____

41   Illustrations of this verse can be found in 1 Kings 18.4 and 2 Kings 4.1-37.

42   The expression "one of these little ones" was often used by the Jewish rabbis or teachers referring to their scholars. So the King likewise refers to His disciples, even to the least of His followers. The reward will be sure, no matter how small the service done to them. Compare chapter 25.40.

Chapter 11

Opposition to the King

In this chapter we find four classes of people who illustrate four attitudes toward the King.

In vs. 2-15 John the Baptizer is loyal-hearted but puzzled.
In vs. 16-19 the crowds are unreasonable and dissatisfied.
In vs. 20-24 the cities are hardhearted and rejecting.
In vs. 25-30 the children (of faith) are trusting and responsive.

1 The instructions of chapter 10 are ended and the apostles have gone out to preach and teach. The King Himself also moves into the towns of Galilee.

The Loyal-hearted Herald, 11.2-15

2 We are reminded that the King's herald had been set aside from active duty, chapter 4.12. John the Baptizer was in prison because he had faithfully preached the message of repentance, even to king Herod. He had told Herod he was sinning and had no right to be living with his brother's wife, Herodias. So Herod put John in prison.

Some Old Testament prophecies had promised the coming Deliverer would be a great Conqueror, bringing vengeance on Israel's enemies, Isaiah 61.1,2; Luke 4.18. John had introduced the kingdom

Matthew 11.1-15

and the King-Messiah. He fully expected the King to reign in righteousness. But now John found himself in prison—for doing right! He probably was wondering why the King had not freed him from prison. As months passed by he heard reports of miracles Jesus was doing.

3 John was still loyal to his Messiah but he was puzzled. Was Jesus really the Coming One, mighty to deliver Israel from Roman power and to set up His kingdom? Even our Lord's disciples expected Him to do so, Acts 1.6. But none of them expected Him to be a suffering Messiah, chapter 16.21,22.

John saw that Jesus was not freeing him from prison, so he sent some of his followers to ask Jesus the direct question: Are You the Coming One? John did the wise thing with his questions and doubts—he sent to Jesus. If we do the same we can be sure He will hear and answer us. We may not be in a prison bodily. Our prison may be a mental one of discouragement, or a spiritual one of doubt. In any case let's learn this lesson from John: take your problems to the Lord Jesus! John's disciples had learned this lesson, too, chapter 14.12. Honest inquiry is always welcomed by our Lord and is always patiently answered.

4 Notice how gracious and understanding our Lord is with John's men. He simply told them to notice what was going on and report it to John.

5 What did they hear and see? Blind people were receiving their sight. This refers to Isaiah 35.5,6 and was one of the important "identity pictures" from the Old Testament. No one had ever opened blind eyes before, but Jesus did. He made the helpless walk, cleansed unclean lepers, opened deaf ears, gave life to dead people, and He preached the Good News to the poor. Here is another "identity picture" from Isaiah 61.1. In Luke 4 He refered to this picture but stopped reading after the first part. He did not read about the day of vengeance of our God. He told the people that the first part (about the day of His favor) was being fulfilled right then. But vengeance and judgment would come later.

So John must learn that the Coming One was first going to suffer and then later would reign as King.

6 This is the happy result of faith. It looks beyond the circumstances and does not stumble over them. Faith hears the Lord say: Trust Me when you cannot trace my ways. That is, believe even if you cannot understand.

7-15 Now the King defends and praises His servant. Some of the crowd may have thought John was a failure. Otherwise why was he left in prison? Or some might think John had lost his faith. The King here gives a wonderful tribute to His herald.

7-10 As John's disciples left, the King asked the crowd three questions. What did they expect to see, a reed of grass swaying in the breeze? Or a man dressed in costly, fancy clothing? No, such are found in king's palaces not in the desert nor in prison. Did they see a prophet? Yes, and the King called him more than a prophet. Then He quoted from Malachi 3.1. This is another "identity picture" of the herald of the King, sent by God to prepare His way.

11-15 The King points out John's true greatness.
   1. *A Great person —*
       (1) Old Testament prophets foretold him.
       (2) He was a prophet, a messenger from God.
       (3) He was greater than all other prophets.
       (4) He not only foretold the King, he **saw** Him.
       (5) He introduced the King in person. Other Old Testament prophets wrote, "The King is coming—look **for** Him." John could say, "Here He is—look **at** Him."

2. *Great firmness*—not easily shaken: (1) by popularity. John didn't "tickle people's ears" by smooth talk; (2) nor by Herod's anger. John didn't "water down" his message to gain favor.

3. *Great courage.* John fearlessly spoke to crowds. He boldly told soldiers what to do. He challenged tax collectors. He preached repentance right in Herod's wicked court. See Luke 3.

4. *Great self-denial.* He lived a simple, rugged life, no fancy clothes.

5. *Great humility.* He didn't seek great things for himself. He gave all glory to his Master. Read John 3.27-30.

6. *Great martyrdom.* He was going to lose his life for the sake of obeying the word of his King.

The King says that no other person of Old Testament history was greater than John, not even Abraham or Moses or David. None were as devoted to God nor had as honored a task as John.

In our day we know the work of Redemption has been completed. Christ has died and risen again and has gone back to heaven glorified. John did not know these wonderful truths. Believers today (even the "lesser ones" v.11) are in a much more wonderful position than John — we are accepted in Christ (Ephesians 1.3. Also see Ephesians 3.4-10).

12 But John had done a good work. Ever since his preaching there had been a turning to God, men and women wholeheartedly, eagerly pressing their way into the kingdom. An illustration of this is in Luke 5.18-20. Also look up Philippians 3.12-16.

13,14 John was the last of the Old Testament prophets. The King refers to another Old Testament passage, Malachi 4.1-5, concerning Elijah's coming. John the Baptizer's coming fulfilled this prophecy.

15 When the King had important things to say He often used the words *He who has ears to hear—listen!* That is, Pay attention to what I say. Look up such places: two times in chapter 13; twice in Mark 4; once in Luke 8 and Luke 14; four times in Revelation 2 and three times in Revelation 3.

The Changeable Crowd, 11.16-19

16,17 The King used an illustration to describe the people of Israel of His day. We have all watched little children at play. They easily move from one toy or game to another. Here they are pretending a make-believe wedding, playing their make-believe flutes and singing "Here comes the bride." But their playmates don't want to play wedding; they refuse to "dance with joy."

So the children change their "game plan" and begin to play that one of them is "dead" and they are at the funeral. They try to look sad and even begin wailing and beating their breasts like the big persons do. But the playmates only turn away and leave. They just can't be satisfied.

18 Now the people around Jesus were just like that. When John came he was a "loner," he didn't attend all the parties and dances in town. No drinking, banquets or reveling for him. Nor did he seek to be popular, number one man in town. He simply preached the message of God. What was the response of the people? Some followed him but many said that he had a demon, that he was crazy.

19 But the Lord Jesus came as the Son of Man, the Royal One. (Do you remember notes on chapter 8.20?) He came as Friend of sinners, to seek and save the lost. He accepted invitations to weddings, John 2.2, and feasts, Luke 5.29. He associated with all kinds of people, Luke 15.1,2. What was the result now? They said Jesus was a glutton and drunkard! This was NOT true. Jesus never ate too much, chapter 4.2, and He was never drunk. They were the empty words of false-minded sinners who hated Him. But what **was** true of their words? He was the Friend of sinners, one of the most beautiful titles He has! Many of us praise His name for it. If He were friend of good people only, we would be left out, Romans 3.10-12. But Friend of sinners—that takes me in, Hallelujah!

The wise children of the King show their wisdom by their actions. They turn from the foolishness of unbelief to trust, love and obey HIM.

The Hard-hearted Rejectors, 11.20-24

20 The King turns to another class of people, those of three cities where many miracles had been performed. Response? No repentance.

21 Chorazin was about two miles north of Capernaum. The Bible doesn't record any miracles there. The Lord performed many miracles we don't read about. The Holy Spirit has chosen to record only certain things for certain reasons. Compare John 20.30,31.

The King says, "Woe to you" that is, how sad and terrible for you. He used this term at least 13 times in Matthew. It is not harsh criticism but rather the wail of pained love wrung from the greatest heart of love in the universe.

Woe, how terrible for you, Bethsaida! Bethsaida was also near Capernaum, like a suburb containing the fishing quarters. It may have been like a twin city with the river Jordan flowing through and between them where it flows into the Sea of Galilee. It was the home of Peter, Andrew and Philip, John 1.44; 12.21. Here a blind man was healed, Mark 8.22; sick ones were healed, Mark 6.45-56. Near here 5,000 were fed, Luke 9.10; and, no doubt, many other unrecorded miracles were also performed here.

But why the sad cry of the King? In spite of all the wonderful blessings poured on them, they refused to repent. Tyre and Sidon were cities on the Mediterranean coast. They did not have the privileges Chorazin and Bethsaida had. If they had, the King says, they would have repented in dust and ashes. (See Jonah 3.5-9).

22 Therefore Tyre and Sidon will be the less severely punished.

23 He turns to Capernaum, an important center in those days. Jesus made His home there for some time, chapter 4.13. Evidently the people were very proud of themselves. The King had performed many miracles there including: healing a nobleman's son, Matthew 8; Matthew lived there and was converted, chapter 9; Peter's wife's mother healed and many others, chapter 8.14-16; an unclean spirit was cast out, Mark 1.23; the daughter of Jairus was raised from the dead, Mark 5, and evidently many others. Again, what was the result? They refused to repent, so they too would be cast down from their pride. If Sodom had seen and heard the Lord Jesus it would have repented and would not have been destroyed.

24 This illustrates a very important Law for all peoples: the greater the light—the greater the responsibility. The more often a person refuses to believe the Good News the greater his punishment will be. So, dear reader, beware how you respond to the King, vs. 28,29.

Matthew 11.20-28

Those Who Respond and Trust, 11.25-30.
Here is the fourth class of people — believers.

25 Four times we read that the Lord Jesus spoke to His Father aloud and publicly; in this verse, in Luke 23.34 and in John 11.41 and 12.27,28. Twice He thanked and praised His Father and twice He made requests. Notice the title He uses here: Lord of heaven and earth. He praises His Father for two things: (1) He has hidden the truth about salvation from mere human wisdom and education. Studying science and philosophy will not teach you about salvation. (2) He revealed His truth to the little children of humility and faith, 18.3; 19.13.

In other words, those who are wise in their own eyes are proud and self-sufficient. But they are nothing in the presence of the Lord of heaven and earth. On the other hand believers are like little children in that they know their weakness and dependence. By faith they are ready and willing to receive true wisdom from God, James 1.5,17.

26 *Yes, Father*: the sign of true submission. Contrast saying NO to the Lord! This believers should never do, as in Matthew 16.22.

27 Here are three important statements by the King: (1) The Father has committed all things to the Son. Here is perfect equality of Father and Son. Compare John 3.35; 5.27; 10.15; 13.3 and 17.2. All authority is included, chapter 28.18. The Son is the Administrator of the Kingdom. (2) Only the Father knows the Son. No one else can fully understand how God the Son and Son of Man are one Person, with God the Father and God the Spirit dwelling in Him. (3) Only the Son fully knows the Father, John 8.55; 17.25. But He did not stop there. If He had, God would be unknowable. But He added that He is known to those to whom the Son chooses to reveal Him! We can know God. How?

28 To whom does the Son choose to reveal the Father? We have already seen that it is not to the "know-it-alls" of earth, but to the little children of faith. Here He defines them—**all** who are weary and burdened with sin and who respond to His invitation; to them He will fully reveal the Father, John 17.6,26.

Here then is the ROYAL INVITATION to all mankind:

The Invitation — Come
The Direction — Unto Me, the Prince/King of Peace
The Invited Ones — All - great and small; no racial barriers nor age limits
Laborers - with restless hearts, Isaiah 57.20,21
Burdened ones - with heavy load of sin

The Promise: I — the Person, the King Himself
   will give — the Promise unfailing
   you — the Personal provision
   Rest — of conscience and soul, vs. 28,29; Isaiah 32.17; Romans 5.1.

29 Here is the challenge to discipleship. *Take up my yoke, learn from me.* Learn to know God the Father, learn to know peace and rest. All from HIM our gracious King. He is gentle and humble, Philippians 2.7,8. For the soul there is rest, peace, refreshment.

30 *My yoke is easy* (well fitting) *and My burden is light.* What is His yoke and what is His burden? His burden would suggest His life-passion: doing His Father's will, perfect obedience to His Father, John 4.34; 8.29. His yoke speaks of His Lordship, we submit; Partnership, we go together, doing the Father's will. See 1 John 5.3.

> I heard the voice of Jesus say,
> Come unto Me and rest,
> Lay down, oh weary one, lay down,
> Your head upon My breast.
> I came to Jesus, as I was,
> Weary and worn and sad,
> I found in Him my resting place,
> And He has made me glad.
>
>   (H. Bonar)

Chapter 12

The King Greater than All

In this chapter we learn more about the King's greatness in five ways.
1. He is greater than the Sabbath, vs. 1-13;
2. He is greater than the Temple, vs. 5,6;
3. He is greater than Satan, vs. 22-29;
4. He is greater than Jonah, vs. 38-41;
5. He is greater than Solomon, v. 42.

        Greater purpose,
        Greater priesthood,
        Greater power,
        Greater preacher, and
        Greater prudence or wisdom.

At the same time we find increasing hatred from His enemies.

Greater than the Sabbath, 12.1-14

First in the grainfield, vs. 1-8, then in the synagogue, vs. 9-14, the Pharisees challenged the King regarding keeping the Sabbath.

1   Jesus and His hungry disciples were walking through grainfields on the Sabbath. As they walked they stripped off ripe heads of grain, and ate the grain, Luke 6.1.

2   The Pharisees told Jesus that His disciples were breaking the law of the Sabbath. Jews were not allowed to do work on the Sabbath (7th day) according to the Law of Moses, Exodus 20.8-11. Jews **were** allowed to pick a handful of grain to eat along the road, Deuteronomy 23.25. And of course they were allowed to eat meals on the Sabbath. But the Pharisees claimed the disciples were breaking the law.

3,4   So Jesus called their attention to what David had done in 1 Samuel 21.1-6. Read this story. The Bread of Presence is mentioned in Exodus 25.30; 40.23; Leviticus 24.5-9. Yet David was not judged for wrongdoing. So neither should the Lord's disciples be judged.

5   Priests performed work on the Sabbath day as they served God in the temple, Numbers 28.9,10. Yet they were innocent of breaking the law of the Sabbath. They worked under a higher law.

7   The King then quoted from Hosea 6.6. They should learn the real meaning of the law: God wants mercy not sacrifice. He values loving response and not just heartless, automatic going through ritual —doing or not doing certain things on certain days. LOVE (and mercy) is the fulfilling of the law. See Romans 13.9,10.

8   Jesus made a startling claim—the Son of Man is LORD of the Sabbath! As Master of the Sabbath He has the right to do with it whatever HE willed to do.

9-12   He showed this authority in the synagogue. A man was there with a crippled hand. The Pharisees challenged Jesus in order to have a case against Him, *Is it lawful to heal on the Sabbath?* He answered them from their own experience. Why would they hurry to rescue one of their own sheep from a pit on the Sabbath? Because they valued their own property.

Jesus loves and cares for HIS property. This man was worth much more than a sheep. The King had the right to do good to HIS man on HIS day. So Jesus healed the man's hand, v. 13.

14   But the Pharisees did not care about the man. They were breaking the "law of mercy" of Hosea 6.6, and they further broke the law by plotting to kill Jesus. How sad! They hated the Lover, despised the Healer, and would kill the Life-giver. They would have mercy on a sheep but not on a man.

Greater than the Temple, 12.5,6

The temple was a beautiful building of which the Jews were very proud. It was the center of their national and religious life. It was destroyed in A.D. 70. Jesus claimed to be greater than the temple. Although He was killed, He arose and still lives on, chapter 28.

However, He probably referred more to the priesthood and sacrifices of the temple. He was greater than that whole order of worship. The reader should read the book of Hebrews, especially chapters 7 to 10. There you will find many ways in which Jesus is greater than that system. See how many you can find and make a list of them.

The Chosen Servant of God, 12.15-21

15   Verse 14 points to Israel's definite rejection of the King, and we now see Him leaving them. Many of the common people believed Him while rejection came from their leaders and rulers, Mark 12.37.

16   As He healed sick ones He told them not to tell others about Him. Why was that? Are we not told to preach about Him to all the world? Yes, now we are. But at that time He did not want publicity. On earth He never looked for popularity. He never "entertained" the

people nor put on a show for mere curiosity. He looked for FAITH.

17-21 Here we find another "identity picture," Isaiah 42.1-4. He is the true Servant of the Lord—chosen, delighted in, v.18 and Spirit-controlled, v.18; not arguing, v.19; merciful, gentle, v.20. The bruised, bent reed pictures mankind as unreliable, undependable. The smoking, smoldering lamp-wick—undesirable, smelling bad. Both would be thrown away by most of us. But not so with the King. He deals in grace with the worthless and useless. He redeems and makes new beings out of lost sinners.

21 In the future He will be the Victorious One, bringing justice to this earth. Now the Gentile nations come into view. They will be (and are now) brought into the blessing of the Lord through this glorious Servant of God, our King.

Greater than Satan, 12.22-29

22 The Sick Patient - his case history:
—condition, blind and unable to talk.
—cause, demon possessed
his cure — Jesus healed him

23 The Surprised People
—astonished, amazed, and asking: could this be the Son of David (Royal title)?

24 The Sullen Pharisees - their hasty explanation:
by Beelzebub, prince of demons (see ch. 10.25)

25-29 The Sure Principle given in reply:
The Person — God Himself who knew their thoughts
The Principle — divided house or kingdom will fall.

Two unanswerable questions: (1) how can such a kingdom stand? (2) how can your sons (fellow Jews) cast him out? (Historians tell us that several prominent Rabbis claimed to cast out demons.)

The Proof — Jesus overcame demons by God's Spirit.

The Picture/Illustration. The strong man is Satan, the god of this age, 2 Corinthians 4.4. The Stronger One is the King Himself. (1) He first tied him up, defeated him at the temptation, chapter 4. (2) He robbed his house — cast out demons, snatching victims from his grasp. (3) He will carry off his possessions. See Isaiah 49.24-26; Hebrews 2.10-15.

30 Summary: the Gatherer is our King; the scatterer is Satan.

Warning, 12.31-37

Now the King warns against speaking against the Holy Spirit. To blaspheme is to revile, rail on, slander, speak evil of, defame. These are all ways in which the word is translated in our English Bible. It speaks of **total rejection**. Verse 24 has just given us an illustration of this. It is unbelief denying the evidence of the Deity of Christ.

31,32 Every kind of sin can be forgiven the repentant heart. The precious blood of Jesus is sufficient to wash away all kinds of sin, 1 John 1.7; 1 Corinthians 6.9-11. But to reject God's provision is fatal. There is no other forgiveness, no salvation.

33 The root produces the fruit. Bad roots (unbelief) produce bad fruit (evil acts).

34,35 The heart is the root, the source. The fruits are the words and decisions. The heart is the storehouse. The treasure or evil comes from inside.

36 The careless word comes out without thinking ahead carefully. It is the index to what is in the heart. Idle, thoughtless talk may seem unimportant to us, but we all must give account for **every** word we speak, at the great judgment day. Because our words flow from the heart, they are the basis for our being found guilty or innocent. God has accurate record of every word ever spoken by every human being.

Greater than Jonah, 12.38-41

It would be good, if our reader has time, to read the book of Jonah just now. It will take only a few minutes.

38 Again the Pharisees come up with the empty request of curiosity: show us a sign, some showy miracle, a dazzling display.

39 But we have already seen that Jesus is not interested in entertaining sinners. He came to save them! In this case He knew their hearts, they were only bent on catching Him (as v. 10). He knew their plan to kill Him, v.14, so He spoke very strongly to them. They already had a sign from Jonah, and no new one would be given them.

40 The sign was Jonah's experience, three days and nights in the belly of the big fish. Here we find the great preacher, Jonah, with the great experience, three days and nights inside the fish (a picture of the death, burial and resurrection of Christ, v.40), preaching a great message, *repent!*, to a great city, Nineveh, with great results, the whole city and the king repented. But there is great judgment on all who reject Christ. The greater Preacher and Prophet is our King.

Matthew 12.31-45   83

Greater than Solomon, 12.42

Here again, if possible, take time to read 1 Kings 10.1-13. It is the story referred to now by the King. The queen of the South (Sheba) heard about Israel's famous king, Solomon. She took a great journey (hundreds of miles/kilometers to Jerusalem), with a great desire, to hear his wisdom. She received great blessing. But there will be a great judgment on all Christ rejectors, because a Greater One than Solomon is here.

In both of these stories the King warns the Pharisees that the men of Nineveh and the Queen of Sheba will stand as witnesses against unbelieving Israel in the judgment day. It all reminds us again that much privilege brings much responsibility.

For the diligent Bible student we suggest you read the story of Solomon in 1 Kings 1-11. See how many ways you can find in which our Lord Jesus is greater than Solomon. For example, his wisdom, 1 Kings 4.29-34, compare Colossians 2.3 and 1 Corinthians 1.30. There are at least seven other ways in which He is greater.

Another Warning, 12.43-45

Now the King illustrates the danger of merely pretending to repent. It is possible to reform the outward life only, which is like painting the outside of a rotten, old building. It may look nice on the outside but it is rotting and decaying inside.

You may chase away the evil spirit of some bad habit or sin but nothing better and positive replaces it. You will be worse off than before. The key word is "empty." Nature resists a vacuum, both in the world around and inside us.

This section illustrates Hebrews 10.26,27 and 2 Peter 2.20-22. It is true of individuals, but it also refers specially to the nation of Israel. They reformed, turned from idolatry, after the captivities, but they rejected their Messiah-King. Being empty they have been subject to God's punishment for centuries. And, worse yet, they will be taken over by the Antichrist in future days, see chapter 24. "This generation" speaks of national Israel as responsible before God, verses 34,39,41,42,45.

The King's Spiritual Family, 12.46-50

The King was interrupted in His teaching. His mother (Mary) and brothers (Mary's sons after Jesus had been born) wanted to talk with Him. Mark 3.20,21 and 31 explain what they wanted to do. This gave Jesus the opportunity to publicly announce the formal cutting of family (human and national) ties, and the binding of the more important spiritual ties.

Salvation is apart from earthly relationships, John 1.12,13; 1 Corinthians 15.50. Discipleship is the same, chapter 10.36; 19.27-29. Our spiritual relationship to the King is the most precious and lasting. Even Mary though highly blessed among women, is no more precious to our Lord than any other believer, as we learn from verse 50.

Chapter 13
The Kingdom in Parables

Now the King gives eight parables, or story-pictures, which describe the progress of the Kingdom of Heaven during the present age.

First we will look at His reasons for using story-pictures in verses 10-17. Then we will look at the eight pictures, one by one.

Reasons for Parables, 13.10-17

10-12 The secrets of the Kingdom were given to the disciples but not to others. The reason is Faith. The disciples had believed the King's words, the others had not. Faith would receive more light while unbelief would lose even what it seemed to have.

13-15 In fact the King quoted from Isaiah (6.9,10) who had foretold this would be the case. The key words are, "They have closed their eyes." They had seen plenty of evidence that Jesus was the promised Deliverer, but they **would** not believe so they turned against Him. Note again chapter 11.20,23; 12.14,24,45.

16,17 Concerning the teaching of the kingdom, the disciples were blessed with more understanding than many Old Testament men were.

Now let's look at the story pictures in order. Note the first four are given to the crowds by the lakeside, v.1,2. The rest are given in the house to the disciples, only, v.36.

1. The Parable of the Sower, 13.3-9,18-23

The first two parables are explained by the King Himself. (A chart in the Appendix may be helpful in understanding the overall view of these parables.) The beginning of the Kingdom was in the preaching of God's Word. This is the first parable. The **results**, through the rest of this present age, are seen in the remaining parables.

1. The Man is a Sower. He is the Son of Man, our Lord Himself, vs.3,37.

2. The Seed is the Word of God, the Good News, v.19; Luke 8.11.

3. The Soils are four responses to the Good News. Note three enemies busy:

(1) The Hard Heart of Rejection, vs. 4,19. These hear but do not receive. Seed does not enter hard ground. It is snatched away by the birds. These picture Satan, v.19, and his evil workers. See Genesis 15.11; 40.17 and Acts 10.12. The enemy is the Devil. Illustration in Luke 7.30.

(2) The Shallow Heart, vs. 5,10-21. The rocks prevent seed from sinking deeply into the soil, so there is no real root. In popular excitement such people say quickly, Oh, yes, I believe all about the Good News. But the hot sun of trouble or persecution soon makes them wither and give up. They hear and rejoice but do not OBEY the Word. The enemy here is the Flesh. Illustration: John 6.66.

(3) The Half-hearted on thorny soil, vs. 7,22. These hear and seem to understand but they allow the things of this world to choke out the Word. Cares of life and love of riches can easily do this. Here the enemy is the World (and its riches). Illustrations: the rich young ruler, Matthew 19.16-24; Demas, 2 Timothy 4.10; Judas, John 12.4-6; Matthew 26.48; 27.5.

(4) The Honest-hearted—Good soil, vs. 8,23; Luke 8.15. These hear, understand and **believe**. The soil has been prepared by the plow and harrow of the Holy Spirit. Rocks and thorns have been removed, and there is fruit in various measure. Some parts are more responsive than others. Illustrations: Eleven disciples out of 12 (91%). At Pentecost 3,000 (60%?); Acts 16.14 Lydia (30%?).

So the Kingdom began as the Word was preached. The results were not very large as rejectors far outnumber believers. It is a picture of the whole age. Some people think of the Good News as a mighty flood overflowing and converting the whole world by the end of the age. But the King did not—He saw the reality.

Consider this parable again: Of one pound of seed sown—perhaps
25% fell on hard ground — Fruit = 0% germination
25% fell on stony ground — Fruit = 0% germination

25% fell on thorny ground — Fruit = 0% germination
25% fell on good soil — Fruit = germination 25% of whole.

Of this last 25%,
33% produced 100 fold, or about 8 pounds
33% produced 60 fold, or about 4.8 pounds
33% produced 30 fold, or about 2.4 pounds
Average total fruit perhaps 15 pounds.

So believers should not be discouraged if there seems to be little fruit. The King sowed anyway and is still sowing the Word by means of His servants today. So keep on sowing! Galatians 6.9.

2. Parable of the Weeds, 13.24-30,36-43

As soon as the King has sown the Good Seed His enemy starts his work also. Here he begins his imitation of the real thing. This parable continues the story of the first parable.

1. The Sower is the Son of Man again, v.37
2. The Field is the world, v.38
3. The Good Seed represents the scattered believers in the world, v.38
4. The night time is the present age, (Romans 13.12. Darkness characterizes evil and evil doers, see John 3.19.)
5. The enemy is the Devil, vs.3,9, deceitful, sneaking in the dark.
6. The weeds are followers of the Devil, v.38. This weed is called Darnel which looks and grows like wheat but is a weed-imitation. It cannot be used with wheat because it is poisonous.

When the King's servants discovered the weeds they were shocked, v.27. But the King knew this was the enemy's work, v.28. The weeds were not to be pulled out until harvest time when they had come to full head. Then the good would be separated from the bad.

7. The harvest is the end of the age, v.39.
8. The reapers are the angels, v.39.

History tells us how true this picture is. Even in New Testament times the weeds began to appear. False prophets and teachers were mentioned by our Lord, Matthew 7.15; by Paul, 2 Timothy 2.17,18; by Peter, 2 Peter 2.1; by John, 1 John 2.18,22,23; by Jude, vs. 3,4. Read these verses and then look around and see how many false cults and religions there are today. They are almost too many to count! Many of them use Bible verses to support their claims but they twist the Scriptures wrongfully, 2 Peter 3.16. Some deny that Jesus is the Son of God. Some claim their own books are as important as the Bible. Others do not even believe in God. All are the result of Satan's deception. He is a liar and the father of lies, John 8.44. Their teachings are like the darnel—poisonous. Beware of them.

So alongside of true Christians there are many false professors. They talk about their church and their religion but they are products of Satan. They will be around until the end of the age, vs.30,39. Then the true believers (wheat) will be gathered safely in God's storehouse (heaven), v.43. But the false teachers and their followers (darnel) will be thrown into the fire of judgment, vs. 41,42.

43 The future is bright for those who believe the Good News—they are made right with God. They will enjoy the sunshine of God's love in the Kingdom of their Father forever.

In verses 9 and 43 the King emphasizes how important it is to believe His Word. He says, You have ears, use them! Listen and obey HIM.

3. Parable of the Mustard Seed, 13.31,32

The mustard seed was well known for its small size, chapter 17.20. It was the smallest vegetable seed used in gardens in those days. Here the King adds more information regarding the kingdom growth in this age. Using His explanations of the first two parables we find: the man is the Son of Man; birds are evil agents of the enemy; the field is the world; the seed is the Word of God.

In this story the emphasis is on the smallness of the seed and the greatness of its growth. Usually mustard grew to be a garden shrub about knee high. But at times it grows larger and here it grew large enough for birds to sit in its branches. The point here is that it grew larger than usual and this resulted in something bad. The birds are evil as we have seen. The tree suggests proud power ruling over all. Read about Nebuchadnezzer in Daniel 4. History tells us how professing Christendom began ruling over the State as a world power. The evil birds of pride, lust for power, greed—all are seen in its branches. There is no fruit for God in this. In contrast the King calls His true Church a "little flock," Luke 12.32. Humility is to characterize His followers, chapter 23.11,12. For the present they are to suffer and submit to the hatred of mankind.

So the "big tree" aspect of Christendom is a shelter for Satan's workers who are doing much evil in this present time. But there is no word about cutting the "tree" down. It will remain evil until the end of the age.

4. Parable of the Yeast and the Meal, 13.33

This story reveals the hidden secret of the rapid outward growth of Christendom. Here we find a woman instead of a man, yeast instead of seeds, and meal or flour. None of these appear in the previous stories so we must look to other Bible references for explanations.

1. The Yeast. (1) In chapter 16.6 we find the yeast of the Pharisees. In verse 12 this means their wrong teaching. In Luke 12.1 it refers to hypocrisy—pretending to be good when really not. (2) Chapter 16.6 also mentions the Sadducees who taught wrongly about resurrection, angels and spirits, Acts 23.8. They only "believed what they saw," which is not faith. (3) Mark 8.15 yeast of Herod, his pride and evil heart, Acts 25.23; 26.27,28. (4) 1 Corinthians 5.1-8 yeast in church life—allowing evil men in fellowship. (6) In the Old Testament yeast was not permitted in meal offerings, Leviticus 2.11, nor in certain special feasts, Exodus 12.15-20. From these brief references we can see that yeast often speaks of evil in various forms.

2. The Meal or Flour would remind the disciples of Old Testament references, as Genesis 18.6, Abraham entertaining the Lord; Leviticus 2.1-3 the fellowship offering; and Leviticus 6.15-17, food for the priests. Yeast was **not** to be added.

3. The woman acts secretly and hides yeast in the flour—like mixing dough for bread. This was an evil act because soon the whole dough was full of it and puffed up, see 1 Corinthians 4.18; 5.2; 8.1. This woman reminds us of Jezebel in Revelation 2.20. You should read her story in 1 Kings 21 and 2 Kings 9.7-37.

Some Bible teachers point out that yeast is not always a picture of evil, for example, Leviticus 7.13; 23.17. They feel that the growth of this parable and the previous one both are good. But the previous one showed there is evil in the kingdom (birds), and most often yeast has meaning of evil. So we feel these stories teach that Christendom is growing in impurity as it grows in size. Again the history of the last 1900 years has confirmed this. Many of Satan's servants have worked right inside the church fellowship. They have introduced their false teachings and evil deeds and have defiled whole churches and denominations. That is why we find in the New Testament many warnings to true believers to keep separate from the evil. See 2 Corinthians 6.14-18.

34-36 The four previous parables were spoken to the crowds, out in the open. The King was speaking to those who could see the outward aspects of the kingdom. Now He goes into the house and teaches the next four parables to His disciples, who had faith. To them He presents more of the "inside" picture of the kingdom.

5. Parable of the Hidden Treasure, 13.44

In this story are two figures we have already met: the man is the Son of Man, who seeks and saves the lost, Luke 19.10; the field is the world. Then we find two new figures, a treasure and a price paid. Again we go to other Bible references to understand these.

A treasure is something very valuable. We read of human treasures in Matthew 2.11; 6.19; Hebrews 11.26; and heavenly, Matthew 6.20; 19.21. If the man pictures our Lord, what did HE value as real treasure? Exodus 19.5 tells us of His special treasure: His people Israel. See also Deuteronomy 4.20 and Psalm 135.4. The Lord has specially chosen Israel from among all the nations. Deuteronomy 32.8-10 suggests how He found this treasure. In John 1.10,11 we read how the King came to His own (treasure) but they rejected Him (as their King). Instead they crucified Him. Israel had to be set aside for the present time (Romans 11.25—the mystery). The treasure was hidden in the field again.

But the man, the King, loved and greatly desired to buy back that treasure, so He bought the field (world). This brings us to the price paid. He went (left heaven) and sold all He had to buy the field. This was at Calvary—He "emptied Himself," Philippians 2.7. He "poured Himself out," Isaiah 53.4-10. He "became poor" 2 Corinthians 8.9. What love!

So His sacrificial death was the means of buying the whole universe back to Himself. He died for the whole world, 1 John 2.2. The field is the world. But within the field is that treasure, Israel. He specifically died for that nation (John 11.51) and for the whole world, 1 John 2.2.

6. Parable of the Precious Pearl, 13.45,46

In a sense this may be a part of the previous parable. Some suggest that the treasure of verse 44 is described here as the precious pearl. The man of the other parables is here called a merchant. He is doing the same thing as in verse 44 —paying a great price, all He had, to buy a special treasure. His search reminds us of Luke 19.10 and John 15.16. But He is searching in the market place. The very valuable treasure here is a pearl.

You probably know that pearls are valuable. But they are different from other gems. Gold and silver are metals dug out of the earth. Pearls are not "dead" metals but come from living creatures—the oysters in sea beds. When a little grain of sand gets into the body of the oyster it hurts. The oyster can't take it away so it begins putting thin layers of covering around the hurtful object. Little by little these layers become thicker and after about seven years a pearl is completed. It is the same color and lustre as the shell of the oyster. Perfect pearls are worth very much money and are used to adorn kings and queens and wealthy people.

This is a beautiful picture of believers. What makes us valuable? We were sinners, enemies of the King, Romans 5.10; we hated Him, John 15.24; we injured Him, 1 Timothy 1.13; Isaiah 53.5. But in His grace

He wrapped us up in His love; He covered us with His own beauty, Isaiah 61.10, and life, 1 Samuel 25.29, Song of Solomon 1.15; Ezekiel 16.14. And Ephesians 5.25-27 looks forward to the day He will present His church perfect in beauty.

But why has He done all this? This precious pearl will adorn the crown of the King Himself, to the praise of HIS glory, Ephesians 1.6,12,14. The church is His glorious inheritance, precious to Him because of the great price He paid—all He had! Its beauty is only a reflection of His own beauty.

7. Parable of the Net, 13.47-50

This pictures the end of the age, verse 49. Here the Man (King) is not in view. But His servants are mentioned, the angels, verse 49. Angels have been serving the King all during our present age, helping believers in various ways, Hebrews 1.14. But they have been working out of sight, unseen by humans. At the end of the age they will be sent to act openly in human affairs. They bring judgment on all who are left on earth at the end of the age, separating wicked from good.

So the treasure represents Israel, and the pearl the church; this leaves only Gentile nations to be dealt with at the end. We suggest this is taught here, but not in full details. More will be seen in chapters 24 and 25.

This parable only outlines the fact that the great net has drawn people from the sea of nations (Gentiles) but who have never been born again. Angels will throw all such into fiery judgment where there is weeping and pain, vs. 41,42. What a warning—sure, awful judgment is coming for all who are not right with God.

Parable of the Householder, 13.51,52

Seven parables have given us a brief outline of the kingdom of heaven. Now, separate from these, the King briefly teaches about responsibility of His followers.

The disciples said they understood the previous parables. So He told them to teach others the truths they had learned. They were like very rich landowners with storerooms full of rich treasure. They were to take out these treasures and share them freely with all around, chapter 10.8. We must share the Good News with our world in our day, Mark 16.15. There are treasures in both Old and New Testaments. We are to preach the whole Word of God, Acts 20.27.

The King returns to Nazareth, 13.53-58

This is a sad paragraph. The King grew up in Nazareth. He preached in the old synagogue there at the beginning of His public service, with words of grace, 4.16-21, and truth, 4.23-27. All the people were angry with Him and tried to push Him over the cliff.

Now, two or three years later, the King returned to His hometown and again entered the synagogue. Old neighbors were there and men He had grown up with. It was like an old town reunion. They had heard about His miracles, now they listened to His words. But we see three wrong things here: (1) Their wrong attitude, they saw Him only as the carpenter's son, not God's Son; (2) This led to a wrong conclusion—they were surprised and stumbled, they should have worshiped; and (3) wrong response: unbelief. Local rejection was a step toward national rejection. He was dishonoured by His own people and family, John 1.11, and 7.5.

The result: no miracles. Unbelief always hinders blessing.

Chapter 14

The Power of the King

The King's Herald Murdered, 14.1-12

1 Herod Antipas was the ruler of one quarter of the Roman province of Syria. He was a son of Herod the Great who ruled when Jesus was born, Matthew 2.1,19. Word has now come to the palace that a great miracle Worker was doing many wonderful things.

2 Herod told his servants that this must be John the Baptizer risen from the dead. He said that because his conscience had been troubling him greatly, and for good reason!

3,4 Some months before this Herod had arrested John and put him in prison. Why? Because John had faithfully preached the King's message: Repent and turn from your sins. Herod had been living in sin with his brother Philip's wife, Herodias. John had bravely told them that they were breaking God's law, Exodus 20.14; Leviticus 18.16, 20.10,21. They had no right to be living together. Of course neither Herod nor Herodias liked to hear that.

5 Herod would have killed John right away, but he was afraid the people would rise up in protest. But Herodias determined to get rid of John anyway.

6,7 Her chance came at Herod's birthday party. She arranged for her own daughter to dance for the wicked king. The banquet hall was filled with important military men and civil servants. When they were well drunk with wine she performed her dance. It was a great success. Herod shouted, Well done! What reward can I give you, up to half my kingdom—you just name it!

8-11 Herodias had given the answer to the girl: the head of John the Baptizer on a platter, and right now! Herod was startled back to sober senses. What should he do? He saw all the guests looking at him; he remembered his promise. But he hated to put John to death, he knew he was a good man. But he went against his conscience and ordered John to be put to death. See Mark 6.20,21.

So the life and service of the King's herald was suddenly ended. But the pangs of Herod's conscience did not end, v.2, nor will they ever end. Nor Herodias', nor her daughter's. All were guilty of murder and will suffer forever for their awful sin, Revelation 21.8.

12 John's disciples buried the body and turned to the Lord Jesus who could truly comfort them in their sorrow. He knew that His own death lay ahead of Him. John's rejection pictured His own.

Five Thousand Fed, 14.13-21

13,14 Jesus withdrew to a quiet, lonely place on the other side of the Sea of Galilee. But crowds followed Him, walking around the end of the lake. Jesus had pity on the many sick ones and He healed them.

15-17 He also knew they were hungry. Since it was getting late the disciples nervously urged Him to send the crowds away to get food. But Jesus told them to feed the people. Of course they didn't have enough food for over 5,000 people.

18-21 And yet they **did** have enough. Five loaves of bread and two fish in the disciples' hands was **not** enough. But in the King's hands it was more than enough. He took the bread and fish, thanked His Father in heaven, broke it and handed it to the disciples. The whole crowd had all they could eat. Twelve handbaskets were left over (for the disciples?). Everyone was more than satisfied.

What a lovely picture of the Good News! Needy sinners receive the bread of life and eternal life through Christ, John 6. No one need go away hungry. All who receive are satisfied, Psalm 107.9. Have you received Him?

Walking on the Water, 14.22-36

John (6.14,15) tells us that the crowds were very excited about how the Lord fed so many people so easily. They said that He must be the Prophet-Deliverer they were looking for. Let's make Him our king right now! But Jesus knew that He must suffer and die before He could reign as King.

22,23 That is why the King sent the crowds back home. Then He sent His disciples in the boat to cross the sea while He Himself went up into the mountains to pray alone.

24-26 As the disciples were crossing, a storm suddenly swept down on them. They were in trouble. But near daybreak Jesus came to them, walking on the water! Here was another Old Testament "identity picture" to assure them that He was their God. See Job 9.8. But the disciples didn't seem to remember that verse. They only thought they were seeing a ghost and they screamed in terror.

27-31 At once Jesus calmed their fear: Don't be afraid, it is I! What relief they felt. So Peter called out to the Lord: If it is you, tell me to come out there to you. What courage and faith Peter had! Jesus answered at once: COME. It must have pleased the Lord to see how trusting Peter was. So Peter actually walked on the water. As long as he trusted he walked. But when Peter looked away from his Lord he saw the storm. Faith turned to fear, and walking changed to sinking. He would surely drown in such a storm. Or would he? Lord save me, Peter cried. That's all that was needed. At once Jesus grabbed Peter's hand. He was safe—still in the storm and only standing on water, but SAFE in the mighty hand of the almighty Son of God, John 10.28.

Safe am I, in the hollow of His hand;
Sheltered over with His love forevermore.
No storm can harm me — no wind alarm me
I am safe forevermore.

31-33 Gently Jesus rebuked Peter for having so little faith. They climbed into the boat and the storm died down. Look up Psalm 107.29,30. Notice the result: they all **worshiped** Him. They confessed that He was the Son of God. This is the first time He has been called this by men. But they KNEW now. Have **you** confessed that Jesus is the Son of God?

34-36 They landed at Gennesaret. People came from all the countryside to be healed. All who even touched the edge of His clothes were made well. Do you think they had heard about the woman of chapter 9.20,21?

So the King proved Himself to be the Mighty One. In Him we find Satisfaction, vs. 13-21, Safety, vs. 22,23, and Strength, vs. 34-36.

Some Bible teachers suggest this chapter gives an outline (in story form) of the present age. We pass it along for the reader to consider.

1. Death of John the Baptizer suggests the death of our Lord.

2. Offering the bread of life is like preaching the Good News today.

3. The Lord ascends mountain to pray, suggesting His present ministry of intercession for His own, as John 17, in heaven.

4. Disciples in the storm suggests Israel in present distress.

5. Peter by faith leaving the boat represents a faithful remnant true to the Lord.

6. Ship lands safely at harbor as soon as the Lord comes— Israel back in the land again.

7. Multitudes blessed suggests the Millennial reign of Christ.

Chapter 15

The King's Teaching and Miracles

Dirty Hands or Heart? 15.1-20

1 Some other Pharisees and teachers of the law came up from Jerusalem.

2 As they watched the disciples they saw that they were eating food without first washing their hands according to the teachings of the old Rabbis. These had taught that a person must go through a certain ritual of washing hands to be ceremonially clean. They taught that a demon named Shibta sat on the hands of men as they slept. So it was necessary to ritually wash hands before eating, otherwise the demon would pollute the food and they would be harmed! Such untrue ideas, mixed with superstition, were given to the people as rules and regulations. See Mark 7.1-4.

And, even worse, those old Rabbis had taught that these rules and teachings were **more** important than God's Word. Here is a sample: "The words of scribes (Rabbis) are lovely above the words of the Law (of God); for the words of the Law are important and unimportant; but the words of the Rabbis are **all** important." And another one: "The words of the elders are weightier than the words of the prophets."

Today there are false teachers who are doing the same thing. They claim their books and teachings are equal to or greater than God's Word, the Bible. And some claim that they are the only ones who should explain God's word to us. We must beware of all such.

3-6 The Lord asked them why they disobeyed **God's** commands by their wrong teaching. Then He gave an example. The law of Moses said we should respect our parents, Exodus 20.12. Whoever cursed parents must die, Exodus 21.17; Leviticus 20.9. This was **God's law**. But the old Rabbis taught that if a person didn't want to support his parents he could dedicate the money to God, calling it a gift (Corban), Mark 7.11. Then he was not responsible to help his parents. This made God's word empty. It directly rejected God's authority.

7-9 Then He quoted from Isaiah 29.13 to show what God said about all this. They spoke nice words about God, but their hearts were evil, far away from God. Their outward worship was worthless because they put man-made rules in the place of God's holy Word.

10,11 So the King called the crowd to Him. He explained that "unclean" refers to spiritual not physical. Washing the outside of the body, of cups and foods is good for outward cleanliness. But in our hearts, inside, we are unclean before God. Sin in the heart causes unclean thoughts, words and deeds.

12-14 The disciples interrupted Jesus to say that He had hurt the feelings of the Pharisees by what He said. But He replied that the Pharisees were like the weeds we just read about in chapter 13.38-40. They were of Satan and would be judged.

Then He said: Leave them alone: they are blind leading the blind, they will all fall into the pit. Why did Jesus leave them? Because they were rejecting Him and His word. Now He is turning from Israel to the Gentiles. All who reject Him will surely fall into judgment.

15-20 Peter then asked Jesus to explain what He meant about being clean and unclean. So Jesus went over it again. Here we should note that ritual uncleanness would prevent a Jew from entering the temple for worship or festivals. Jesus was referring to spiritual uncleanness of sin in the heart.

The Jews tried to control everything from the outside: wash hands and foods, only eat certain foods, keep the sabbath. It was all outward and physical. But Jesus showed that the heart is the source of our trouble. Verse 19 lists the wrong things which come from inside us. These sins prevent us from entering heaven, see Revelation 21.8. How can we be washed inside? By the blood of Jesus, 1 John 1.7.

What can wash away my sin?
Nothing but the blood of Jesus.

A Gentile's Great Faith, 15.21-28

21 The King left Israel and traveled west to the region of Tyre and Sidon, on the coast of the Mediterranean Sea. This was the Gentile country of Phoenicia, in Syria. He was symbolically "turning to the Gentiles."

22,23 There was a Gentile woman who had a demon-possessed daughter. Perhaps she had heard about Jesus at the time of Luke 6.17. She came to Jesus crying, Lord, Son of David, have mercy on me. But Jesus did not respond, as if He had not heard her. This seems strange, doesn't it? He always was full of pity and love. No one coming to Him for help had ever been turned away. But she kept on begging His disciples to help her. They asked Jesus to send her away, as in chapter 14.15, because they didn't like her bothering them.

24 But Jesus did not send her away. He would not do such a thing. Instead He said that He had been sent only to the lost sheep of Israel. (Do you remember chapter 10.5-7?)

25 When the woman heard that she came to Jesus and knelt down before Him, saying, Lord, help me! She heard that word: lost. She knew it was true of her. He was interested in those who had a need.

Did you notice how she addressed Him? First she said, Son of David. (Do you remember chapter 9.27?) There are six places in Matthew where this title is used. Look up the following chapters, find the verse and write down who used this title: chapters 9, 12, 15, 20, and 21 twice. This woman was not Jewish and had no right to use the strictly Jewish title, Son of David. So she used His general title, Lord. (He is Lord of all, Acts 10.36). Her faith was growing, also her understanding and courage.

26,27 The Lord knew she had faith in her heart. He wanted to draw it out to full measure. So He tested her: It isn't right to throw children's food to dogs. Again she admitted her need. The Gentiles were called dogs by Jews (Psalm 22.16). They were despised and worthless. But her faith grows strong: Even little dogs are in Jewish homes and eat crumbs and scraps from the master's table.

28 Immediately Jesus responds to her great faith: Your request is granted! Faith on the knees of humility receives the blessing of the Lord. The daughter was healed at once.

The King Returns to Galilee, 15.29-31

Officially the King is turning away from Israel the nation. But He still has great love for the individuals. So He returns to the needy ones in Galilee. Up in the hills He sits down and great crowds of sick, lame, blind and crippled come to Him. He heals them all and they praise the God of Israel. The nations' rulers and leaders may reject Him, but He gladly heals individuals with faith.

Four Thousand Fed, 15.32-39

32 They must have been together for three days. Their food was long gone and there were no shops near. The King felt sorry for them and said that He wouldn't send them away hungry.

33,34 The disciples suffered from poor memories. They asked where they could get enough bread to feed such a crowd. Didn't they remember the 5,000 of chapter 14? This time they had seven loaves and a few small fish. Again the bread they had wasn't enough. But in the King's hands it was more than enough.

35-38 Note how orderly the King is. The crowds must sit down. He gives thanks to His Father, divides, and hands to the disciples. They pass on the increasing supply to the hungry crowd. All eat and are satisfied, and go home, 4,000 men plus women and children. No pushing and panic, no elbowing or fighting. A scene of peace and enjoyment: needs met, emptiness replaced by fulness; hunger gives way to satisfaction. Have you experienced this in your life?

Next the King and His disciples got into the boat and went to the area of Magadan, probably Magdala on the west coast of the Sea of Galilee.

Chapter 16

The Great Confession

Four Signs, 16.1-4

1 Again some leaders came to our Lord demanding a sign or miracle from heaven. This time it was Pharisees and Sadducees. He could easily have produced some dazzling display of mighty power. But that wouldn't have convinced them.

2,3 So the King points them to signs of the weather. They were all familiar with the old saying:
> Red in the morning — shepherd's warning;
> Red at night — shepherd's delight.

But they were blind to the more important signs of the times they were living in. These were shouting out to them: Your King is here! Matthew has been recording many of them: blind seeing, lame walking, lepers cured, etc. But they didn't recognize their King.

4 So the King gives them only one other sign—the sign of Jonah the prophet. See chapter 12.39,40. He called them a wicked, evil people because they were willfully rejecting all the evidence that He was truly their promised Deliverer. So He left them and went away.

The Yeast Again, 16.5-12

5 The King and His disciples crossed the lake. But they had forgotten to take food along.

6-11 Jesus told them to be on guard against the yeast of the Pharisees and Sadducees. They thought He was talking about physical bread but He spoke about the evil teaching.

12 The yeast of the Pharisees was their empty, formal religion. They were rigidly applying the "letter" of the law and not its true meaning. For example their Rabbis taught that if an egg were laid on the day after the Sabbath it could not be eaten because it was "prepared" on the Sabbath (see Exodus 16.5). What hypocrites! And they taught that their sayings were just as important as God's Word!

The yeast of Sadducees was unbelief in resurrection, as we have seen before.

And the disciples were wrong in thinking only of loaves of bread instead of spiritual things. So today we should beware of these two things: (1) Any addition to God's Word, the Bible. Some men claim their ideas, visions and dreams are new messages from God to mankind. The Bible is God's completed message to us. (2) Any subtraction from God's Word. Many today are teaching that the Bible is not really all inspired, that we cannot believe the miracles and other parts of the Bible. But they are denying Christ the King when they do so. Beware of such. Read carefully Revelation 22.18,19.

Peter's Confession of Faith, 16.13-16

13,14 The King and His disciples traveled near Caesarea Philippi. There He asked them, "Who are people saying I am?" So they began listing some they had heard:

1. John the Baptizer (chap. 14.1,2). He was God's voice to the people.
2. Elijah (Malachi 4.5). He was bold, fiery and brave.
3. Jeremiah, man of thunder and tears. (Lamentations 1.16)
4. One of the other prophets, with wisdom and understanding.

But they were all wrong. They only saw Jesus as a wonderful **man**. They needed faith in Divine revelation.

15,16 So Jesus asked the disciples, What about you? Who do you say I am? Then Peter spoke for all of them: YOU are the Christ (Messiah), Son of the Living God.

1. Christ is the New Testament word for Messiah in the Old Testament. Both mean the anointed one. Anointed by God, chosen, prepared, sent and blessed by God the Holy Spirit. Jesus is the long-expected Deliverer.

2. The Son—we have already read God the Father's word concerning Him: My Son, My delight, chapters 3.17; 17.5.

3. Of the God—the only true God of the universe, 1 John 5.20.

4. The Living One—our God is the living God and the life-giving God. The title the Living God is found at least seven other times in the Bible. Find them and fill in the verses. Here are some clues:

> Joshua 3 v. ____
> Psalm 42 v. ____
> Jeremiah 10 v. __
> Daniel 6 v. ____
> Acts 14 v. _____
> 1 Timothy 3 v. __
> Hebrews 10 v. __

So Peter makes the great Confession of Faith in the person of our Lord, Savior and King. Jesus is **more** than a carpenter or teacher or healer or example or mere man. He is GOD!

The King's Response, 16.17-20

17 The blessedness of knowing and confessing Jesus as God. Notice the names Jesus used for Peter: **Simon** means listening (Romans 10.17). Son of **Jonah**, which means dove. The dove is a picture of the Holy Spirit (see chap. 3.16). These names tell us that the Holy Spirit, through the hearing of God's Word, reveals Christ to us, John 16.13,14. And through the Spirit the Father had revealed the truth to Peter.

18 The King gave Simon his new name—Peter, which means a stone or small piece of rock. On the Rock (great boulder or bed-rock) Christ was going to build His church. Now we must carefully notice that Christ did not say He would build His church on Peter (as some people teach). Peter means a small stone, and Peter was too weak and failing for Christ to build His church on him. Look at verses 22,23 where Jesus had to address him as Satan. Also read chapter 26.34,69-75. The church needs a more sure and solid foundation than Peter. And it has!

ROCK is a title of God Himself. At least 24 times the Old Testament used Rock in reference to Jehovah-God Himself. For examples see Deuteronomy 32.3,4; 2 Samuel 22.2,3,32; Isaiah 28.16. See if you can find some of the other references. Christ was going to build the church (HIS church) on the Rock Himself, God, the living God, the Son of the living God. That's who "this rock" refers to. Let's look at this prophetic promise:

I—the King Himself is the Architect, Designer and Builder. It is all His plan and purpose, and the product of His great work on the cross, 1 Corinthians 3.11.

will—future tense looks forward to the foundation—at Calvary, and the beginning—at Pentecost. His church is not an extension of Old Testament Israel, but a NEW thing. Ephesians 3.4,5 says it was a mystery, untold secret, before the New Testament was written.

build—not a building of bricks, steel and stained glass. **Believers** are living stones (1 Peter 2.4-8) being built into the spiritual temple, 1 Corinthians 3.9,16.

My—relationship, ownership, by purchase, Acts 20.28. It belongs to HIM, not to any of His servants. It is precious to Him.

Church—the Body of Christ, composed of all true believers. It is His Assembly, His called-out ones, gathered out from the world; His select people, His treasure, His Bride, 1 Peter 2.9; Ephesians 5.23-33. He adds daily to her number, Acts 2.47. He loved her and gave Himself for her, Ephesians 5.23-27. He makes her holy, set apart for

Himself. He will make her perfect. He is her Head, v. 23; Colossians 1.18.

Victorious—It will not be overcome by all the powers of Satan and of death, because it is founded on the Living God, the Living Rock.

The church's one Foundation is Jesus Christ her Lord,
She is His new creation by water and the word.
From heaven He came and sought her to be His holy bride;
With His own blood He bought her and for her life He died.

19 Authority is represented in the Keys. These are given here to Peter as representative of all believers. All believers are included in Matthew 18.18 and John 20.23. So Peter is not more important than any other believer. The keys speak of opening doors. As an individual Peter was privileged to open the door of Good News to Jews at Pentecost (Acts 2) and to Gentiles, at Cornelius' house, Acts 10. But the other Apostles opened doors of preaching in other lands. And all believers today should still be offering Salvation through the Good News into all the world. We preach on the authority of God's Word.

But we suggest also that chapter 13.52 can be applied here. All believers, through the Holy Spirit, should be unlocking and opening the storehouse of spiritual riches of the Bible to share with others.

But what does the "unbinding and loosing" refer to? We suggest it refers to discipline and government in the kingdom of heaven or the church. It surely is not the final authority of forgiving the guilt of a sinner nor of dooming him to hell forever. ONLY the Lord has authority to forgive sins (chapter 9.6; Mark 2.7) or to throw into hell (chapter 10.28). Only HE holds the keys of future judgment, Revelation 1.18.

We must notice that all three references to this (chapter 16.19; 18.18; John 20.23) have important verb tenses. They really tell us that the believers on earth are to bind or loose (forgive or not forgive) according as **has already been done in heaven**. It simply means that believers only **confirm** what Christ in heaven has already done.

Here we might point out a few differences between the kingdom of heaven and the church:

Kingdom of Heaven	**Church**
includes all who **profess** to believe	includes only actual believers
related to earth	related to heaven
under rule of a King	love of a Bridegroom
responsibilities	privileges

20 Verse 20 may again sound strange to us. We have noticed three times before that the Lord told people NOT to tell others about Him, 8.4; 9.30; 12.16. And now Peter has just given his Great Confession of who Jesus really was. Why does Jesus warn them not to tell anyone else? Verse 21 gives the answer.

21 Jesus begins to explain that though King He must suffer before He will reign. He carefully states each step: (1) the necessity—He must go: (2) where—to Jerusalem; (3) why—to suffer; (4) what—many things; (5) from whom—elders, chief priests, teachers of law; (6) result—be killed, and (7) what then?—raised to life!

22,23 None of the disciples were looking for this. Their idea was a Messiah-Deliverer-King to reign right away. Peter speaks for them all: Lord, this suffering shall never happen to you! But Jesus sternly rebuked him—calling him Satan! Satan is the adversary, or enemy, and accuser. Peter was thinking the thoughts of man not of God. In that way he was allowing Satan to try to block the King's path to the cross. So he was acting as a stumbling block to Christ, chapter 4.10; Ephesians 6.12; 1 Peter 2.7,8.

24 The King has seen the increasing rejection and hatred of the rulers. He is now firmly turning His face to the cross, Luke 9.51. He must prepare His followers so He warns them they also have a cross to face. Reigning time will only follow suffering time. Discipleship is training time. Here are the three steps:

1. Deny yourself, that is, forget selfish interests. Say "No" to self. By nature the "I" sits on the throne of our lives. I will do this or that; I run my own life. But we must take self off that throne.

2. Take up the cross. The cross is not a beautiful ornament to be hung around the neck as jewelry or decoration. The cross is an instrument of death, painful and shameful. But this cross is not our Lord's cross—that was Redemption. His suffering was for our sins, and only He could bear that cross. But each believer must take up his or her own cross—of submission. It is the definite choice of the heart, "take up." Not my will but God's will be done.

3. Follow Me, in obedience and devotion to our King; in willing, glad service of loving dedication of all we are and have.

25 The choice is very simple. If we try to save our life for ourselves we will lose it. Living for self ends in a wasted, lost life. Living for Christ is to find and keep life.

Only one life — it will soon be past
Only what is done for Christ will really last.

We have already referred to the five young missionaries who were trying to reach the Auca Indians and were killed by them. Many people at that time said, What a waste of life! But they had **gained** life by laying it down for their King.

26 The King asks two questions: (1) What gain does one have if he wins the whole world yet loses his own life? Can you answer that question? (2) What is worth exchanging your soul, or life, for? Many are making bad exchanges. Here are some who did:

Judas lost his soul for 30 pieces of silver (and lost the silver too!)

Pilate lost his soul for a palace and popularity—and lost both.

The rich young ruler lost his soul for wealth, but he lost his wealth too when he died.

What are you exchanging your soul for?

27 But the King reminds His followers that when He comes again in glory He will bring His rewards for all who faithfully follow and serve Him. For them it will be all gain if they have fulfilled verse 24.

28 He announces a preview of the kingdom glory. Very shortly some of His disciples would be granted a little glimpse of their King in His glory.

Chapter 17

The Glory of the King

The King in His Glory, 17.1-8

1 We have had the Great Confession of Christ's Deity; then the prediction of His sufferings. Now we come to a picture of the glory to follow, Luke 24.26.

2 Jesus was praying on a high mountain, Luke 9.29. His three "specially close" disciples, Peter, James and John, had been invited to go with Him. It must have been a long climb as the disciples were very tired, Luke 9.32. As they dozed they were suddenly awakened to realize something exciting and wonderful was taking place. Jesus was being changed in appearance before their very eyes. His face was glowing like the bright sun itself. His clothing was also shining with bright, beautiful light. What was happening?

Perhaps the disciples remembered the verses in Psalm 104.1,2, "O Lord my God you are very great; you are clothed with glorious majesty. You wrap yourself with light like a garment." They had just confessed that Jesus was the Son of God. Here He was allowing His inner beauty and glory to shine through His body and clothes. They were seeing a little outshining of His heavenly, divine glory. It was a little foretaste of heaven, Revelation 1.12-18.

3 Then they noticed two men with Jesus: Moses the great lawgiver and Elijah the great prophet. Moses had died 1,500 years before, and Elijah had been snatched up to heaven without dying 900 years before. But here they were, alive and well, talking with their Lord and God—Jesus! The disciples knew who they were. What were they talking about? Luke 9.31 tells us they were discussing the death which Jesus was about to fulfill in Jerusalem. Think of that! The conversation of heaven centered around the soon-coming death of the King. Redemption is the central theme of the law (Moses) and prophets (Elijah). Can you think of some Old Testament verses that prove that?

4 Peter spoke for the others, "Lord, it's wonderful to be here. Let Moses and Elijah stay around, and let's build three shelters for you." That is, we would love to stay right here for a long time. Mark and Luke tell us Peter didn't realize what he was saying, he was so frightened and excited.

5   But while he was still talking a very bright cloud came over them. They heard a Voice from heaven: "This is My own dear Son . . . listen to Him, obey Him." The disciples were afraid but they knew what that bright cloud was. It had appeared in the Old Testament at various times. In that cloud the Lord had led their ancestors through the wilderness, Exodus 13.21,22. It had filled the tabernacle and temple at dedication time, Exodus 40.35; 1 Kings 8.10. It represented the very presence and glory of God. The disciples knew Whose voice spoke now.

6   They realized they were in the very presence of God, so they fell down, faces to the ground. No one could be in God's presence and live unless he brought a sacrifice for sin, Hebrews 9.7.

7,8   But Jesus came and touched them, saying, Don't be afraid. Why? The very blood offering required by God was what He and Moses and Elijah had just been talking about. He was going to the cross to shed His blood as the sin offering for mankind, Hebrews 9.11-15. So God the Father glorified the Son. All others must fade away.

Elijah, 17.9-13

9   On the way down the mountain Jesus told His disciples not to tell anyone about this experience until after He rose from the dead. It might have been hard for the disciples to obey, but they did. However they never forgot about it. Many years later Peter wrote about it, 2 Peter 1.16-18. It was a prophetic vision of the coming and power of our Lord.

10   Yes, they knew Jesus was surely the promised Messiah. But they were puzzled about the verses in Malachi 4.5,6. The prophet had written that Elijah would come to earth to turn the people to God just before Messiah would come. So they asked Jesus about this.

11-13   He told them John the Baptizer fulfilled that prophecy. John had come but he had been put to death. He reminded them that He too was going to suffer in the same way.

The Demon-possessed Boy, 17.14-22

14-16   As the four of them got back to the other disciples a man came to Jesus in great distress. He asked the other nine to heal his sick son but they could not. A demon who possessed this poor boy often caused him to fall into the fire or water.

17-19   Jesus was grieved in His heart. It was hard for Him to see the suffering of people, and harder still for Him to see the lack of faith. So He healed the boy by casting out the demon. Afterward the disciples asked Him privately, Why couldn't we heal him?

20,21 The answer was: too little faith. They had all been given power to drive out demons, chapter 10.1. But evidently they had not been exercising their faith. The more we use faith the stronger it grows. Some Bibles add in verse 21 that prayer and fasting were necessary. So it seems they had not been keeping in touch with the Source of power in prayer, nor keeping away from self-pleasing by fasting. Where there is genuine, sincere faith it can move mountains—of sorrow, or of difficulty.

"Nothing will be impossible for you." This word must be linked with "Nothing is impossible with God," Luke 1.37. In Philippians 4.13 Paul could write, by faith, "I can do all things." But he must add, "through Christ who gives me strength." God is able to do anything which is according to His will. Obviously He cannot do what would dishonor Himself. Neither can true faith ask for anything which would be contrary to the character and will of God.

The Sad Reminder, 17.22,23

Back in Galilee Jesus gathered His disciples again. Now dark shadows are increasing over Him. From now on He will be speaking more and more about suffering. He tells them plainly about His betrayal, death and resurrection. This time there is no protest by His followers. Only grief.

Tax Time, 17.24-27

24 Now they are in Capernaum. The tax collectors are around again.

Back in Exodus 30.11-16 and 38.26 God had commanded that redemption money must be paid for all who were entered in the census. That had not been carried out by Israel for centuries. But now in the time of Jesus there was this temple tax, an annual tribute for temple service. The two drachma coin was equal to the half-shekel of the Old Testament.

25 Peter was asked whether his Master paid the temple tax. Peter answered, Yes. When he came into the house Jesus (who knew what Peter had said) questioned him, Does a king put tax on his own children or others?

26 Peter, of course, replied, Others. Then the children don't have to pay, do they? So Jesus reminds Peter and the rest that HE is the King over all and was not subject to tax. He literally owns the whole world—He made it! Who would dare to tax the King and Owner of everything? No one.

But the King was not reigning in glory over the whole world yet. He was in the world, it was made by Him, but didn't know who He was, John 1.10. He was taking the lowly place of rejection.

27 So, although King, He would not stand up for His rights. He would not offend the people, so He tells Peter to hook a fish down at the seashore. In its mouth would be a four drachma coin to pay the tax for them both. What poverty! The King didn't have money enough to pay the tax. Yet what grace— He paid Peter's as well. On the cross Jesus paid our debt in full. What an example. He **paid**. So His followers also pay taxes when they are required to, see Romans 13.6-8.

Chapter 18

Teaching About the Church

Greatest in the Kingdom, 18.1-10

1 The disciples had just been hearing their King speak of His approaching suffering. Yet their hearts seem to be set more on a kingdom of glory. They argued about which of them was going to be the greatest in the kingdom. So they asked Jesus.

2 Jesus called a little child to Him as an object lesson for us all. Here is a simple outline to remember:

Converted, v.3 . See 1 Thessalonians 1.9.
Humble, v. 4. Philippians 2.5-11.
Invited, v.2, called, Come. Matthew 11.28.
Loved, v.5-7, by the Lord.
Dependent, needing help.

Other characteristics of a child: faith, unquestioning confidence, simplicity, 2 Corinthians 11.3, grace, mildness, favor.

3-6,10 Our relationship to a child: We should be like him, in humility; we should welcome him, as we welcome Christ; we should not cause him to sin; we should not despise or belittle him.

6,7 Warnings. It is very dangerous to cause a young believer in Christ to sin. The King said: better to drown than to commit such a sin. It is bad enough to sin ourselves, but to cause someone else to sin is "double trouble" for us. Our Lord lets us know how very much He loves and cares for the children.

8,9 These verses have already been noted in chapter 5.29,30. See notes there.

Matthew 18.1-20

10 To despise one of Christ's little ones is forbidden. He tells us they each have an angel watching over them and they are constantly reporting to God the Father in heaven. See Hebrews 1.14.

Parable of the Lost Sheep, 18.11-14

Then the King illustrates what He means. God the Father sent His Son, Jesus Christ, into the world to seek and to save the lost. We all are like lost sheep. Each of us has gone astray, Isaiah 53.6. But He loves each one of us and looks for the lost ones. Then He rejoices greatly when He finds it, Luke 15.3-7. Even so God the Father is not willing that one little one should perish, 2 Peter 3.9.

Church Fellowship, 18.15-20

Now our Lord talks a little about the church He had mentioned in chapter 16.18. Notice the three times He refers to "two or three": v. 16 regarding church discipline; v. 19, prayer, and v. 20, Body fellowship. These are three aspects of church activities:

1. *Church Discipline*, vs. 15-17. When a believer has sinned against another it should be made right. There are three steps: (1) One meets one, personal meeting between the two. If no success, then (2) One plus one or two meet one, (Deuteronomy 19.15), witnesses to the wrong done, and they attempt to correct it. If still no success then (3) the whole church, or at least church elders meet with the wrongdoer. All is done with a view of making things right. But if the wrongdoer refuses to listen he can only be put out of the church fellowship until he changes his attitude and makes things right. Note 2 Thessalonians 3.14,15.

18 Concerning binding and loosing, see note on chapter 16.19.

19 2. Now we learn about *Church Prayer*. If at least two agree about a request then they should pray. They will be of one mind about it. What they are going to pray for must be: (1) according to the will of God, and (2) according to the Word of God. The pattern is: agree, ask, answered. What an encouragement for us to pray.

20 3. *Church Fellowship*. This includes doing the church business, as discipline, etc. vs. 17,18, prayer, v.19, and worship, v.20. Gathered together means the Holy Spirit draws believers together in the Lord's Name. "In My Name" speaks of (1) possession, they belong to Him; (2) authority, He is the Head of the Body, Colossians 1.18; and (3) identity, no other name, Acts 4.12. Then comes the wonderful promise: I am right there among them. What a precious experience to know the Lord Himself delights to be near His own, in the Center.

There are a number of times our Lord is found "in the midst" or in the center. In the chapters listed find out which verse and write down where the Lord is found:

(Example)
        Luke 2. v.<u>46</u> <u>in temple</u>
        Matthew 18. v. ____ _____
        John 19. v. ____ _____
        Luke 24. v. ____ _____
        John 20. (2) vs. ____ ____ _____
        Hebrews 2. v. ____ _____
        Revelation 1. v. ____ _____
        Revelation 2. v. ____ _____
        Revelation 5. v. ____ _____
        Revelation 7. v. ____ _____

Meditate on these verses, note how wonderful our great Lord and King is: the Central One. He is the All-Sufficient One and the All-Satisfying One. Praise His Name!

A Parable of Forgiveness, 18.21-35

21 No doubt Peter was thinking over what Jesus had said in verse 15.
    He asked how many times he should forgive someone who sinned against him. The old Rabbis taught three times was a proper limit. Perhaps Peter thought seven would be the perfect number.

22 But Jesus said, Not seven but seventy times seven (or some Bibles
    say seventy-seven). In other words there should be no limit to our forgiveness to those who wrong us.

23 Then Jesus gave an illustration. The kingdom of heaven is like a
    king who was going to settle accounts with his servants. One specially favored servant had been loaned a very large sum of money, 10,000 talents. One talent equaled 6,000 days' wages (that is over 15 years' wages). Multiply that by 10,000 and then multiply that by how much money you earn each day. You will then have some idea of how much this servant was in debt.

24,25 When the king wanted the money the man of course couldn't
    pay it. He didn't have it. So the custom was to sell the debtor and his wife and children as slaves. They then would have to work hard all the rest of their lives to pay back at least part of the debt.

26 But the man fell on his knees and begged for more time and
    promised to pay it all back. Imagine such a rash promise. He

wouldn't be able to earn enough in his lifetime even to pay off the interest.

27 The king knew he could never pay it. But he had pity on him and in love forgave the whole debt and let him go free. How very thankful that servant should have been.

28 But was he? No. Instead he looked up another servant who owed him only about 100 days' wages. He grabbed him by the throat and demanded that he pay back what he owed him.

29,30 But the poor fellow couldn't. He begged for mercy, promising to pay back all his debt. But the first servant refused and put him in prison. No mercy or forgiveness. Here is a picture of one who only professes to be a follower of Jesus. We have already read in chapter 6.14,15 about such. He certainly is not a man of faith because faith works by love and without love there is no faith. Read James 2.13 and Proverbs 21.13.

31-33 This servant is called a wicked servant because he showed no love or forgiveness, but only greed and hatred. 1 John 3.10,14,15 show us that such a person is not a forgiven believer but only a false professor. There are many such in the kingdom of heaven. They are not true followers of the King. True followers love because Christ has first loved them, 1 John 4.19.

34 The King is rightfully angry with this man. Instead of being touched by the kindness of his own master he only became more greedy and hardhearted. There was no repentance or change of heart. Only judgment can follow.

35 There will be no mercy on the unforgiving ones. As one Bible teacher wrote, One thing God will not forgive is an unforgiving heart. By contrast look up Luke 7.44-48. The woman who had been forgiven much showed much love. Do you?

Chapter 19
Teaching About the Family
Divorce and Marriage, 19.1-12

1,2 Jesus next went to Judea, across Jordan (east side).

3 Some Pharisees came to ask Him about divorce. During New Testament days Jewish Rabbis were divided between two old teachers, Hillel and Shammai. Hillel taught that divorce could be for "any cause," such as if a woman was not a good cook. But Shammai taught only "one cause"—unfaithfulness to a spouse. It seems the Pharisees here were trying to get Jesus to "take sides."

4-6 Jesus took them right back to the beginning, Genesis 1.27. God's original plan was: one man and one woman married for life. Two became one permanently. In marriage it is 1+1=1. Let no man separate them because God has joined them together.

7,8 The Pharisees asked why Moses commanded a man to give a notice or letter of divorce when he sent his wife away. Jesus corrected them: Moses permitted not commanded—because their hearts were hard in disobedience. (Actually it was a protection from unfair treatment of the women.)

Surely Christians today should not be "hardhearted" about their marital problems. Instead they are to be kind and **tender** hearted to one another, forgiving each other, Ephesians 4.32. Believers today should realize that God wants them to be reconciled not divorced, forgiving not fighting, loving not hating.

9 Then the Lord specifically states that divorce was ONLY for unfaithfulness. Otherwise to divorce and remarry was to commit adultery.*

10-12 The disciples said then that it would be better not to marry. And Jesus replied that there are three reasons why men do not marry: (1) some cannot marry and have children because they were born that way; (2) some, because men made them that way; and (3) some do not marry for the sake of the Lord and His kingdom. That is, they devote their whole lives to serving the Lord and therefore do not marry.

---

*FOOTNOTE: This is a difficult and large subject and space forbids our going into it in more detail here. We suggest the reader obtain *A Biblical History of Marriage, Divorce and Remarriage*, or *Fornication and Divorce*, published by Everyday Publications Inc.

In summary we would add: Better not to marry than to marry the wrong person; better not to marry than to marry against the Lord's will.

Children, 19.13-15

The King **loves** children. But the disciples did not share His love. They must have forgotten His words and actions in chapter 18.2. They were too busy to be bothered and they scolded the parents who brought them to Jesus. But it turned on their own heads. Mark 10.14 tells us that Jesus was angry with **them**. What a loving Savior! He removes the hindrance: do not stop them. He welcomes them in His arms, Mark 10.16. (See the Old Testament picture-prophecy of this in Isaiah 40.11). And He blesses them—laying hands on them, v.15.

Just a word to parents. These parents showed a good desire: to have their children blessed. Parents are responsible to provide for their children's bodies and minds, food, clothing, home, etc. But **far** more important — they are responsible for their children's eternal welfare! Remember, your child is a "little eternity." That is, he is going to last forever and will spend eternity somewhere, in heaven or hell. Be sure you take your responsibility seriously. The parents here were wise—they brought their children to the Right Person. Only He can bless them and give them eternal life. His warning is to all: Never hinder a child, in any way, from coming to the Savior. Do you remember chapter 18.6,7? Read it again.

The Rich Young Man, 19.16-30

16 Now remember the setting: children, in simplicity and humility, coming to Jesus. Of such is the kingdom of heaven. Now comes a rich, young ruler running to Jesus. Notice he had:
1. Good Position—he was a ruler, Luke 18.18,
2. Good Possessions—he was very rich, v.22,
3. Good Hope of life (earthly)—he was young, v.20,
4. Good Intentions—earnest and sincere, seeking eternal life, running, Mark 10.17,
5. Good Manners—polite respectful, "Teacher," kneeling, Mark 10.17.

18-20 6. Good Character, outwardly at least. We would say he was "above average" today. No criminal record, a decent, upright sort of person. He seemed to have lots of good about him.

But Jesus pointed out that the only good person is God. This young man thought of himself as good enough to gain life eternal. He claimed to have kept all the laws mentioned in verses 18,19. See Exodus 20.12-16; Deuteronomy 5.16-20.

21 Jesus did not question his claim, but He must point out what he lacked. He had much but he lacked much more. He lacked eternal life because he was trying to find it, v.16. He lacked satisfaction, v.20. He lacked true "good," v.17. He lacked true riches (treasure in heaven) v. 21. Then Jesus put His finger on this man's problem. He commanded: Share your possessions, then Come, follow ME.

22 This man was self-centered. He lived for himself not his neighbor.

He thought more of his possessions than of his soul's salvation; more of treasure on earth than treasure in heaven, v.21. His choice: instead of coming to Christ he went away from Him; instead of following Christ he went away sad.

23,24 Sadly Jesus gave His disciples an illustration. The old cities had walls around them with large gates which were closed at night. In the big gate was a small door for a man to enter "after hours" without having to open the big gate. But if a late traveler came with his camel the man had to unload the camel. Then the camel could barely squeeze through the small door, called the "needle's eye gate." In such a way a man with great wealth finds it hard to enter Christ's kingdom. Our possessions can hinder us from:

(1) Entering the kingdom, contrast chapter 5.3. Wealth often brings pride;

(2) Enjoying the kingdom, see 1 Timothy 6.6-11; and

(3) Enlarging the kingdom, see 1 Timothy 6.17-19

25-27 The disciples were surprised. They wondered who then could be saved. Of course no one can save himself, only God can save. But the young man chose to cling to his riches and leave the Savior. Then Peter speaks up: They, the disciples, had left everything to follow the Lord. What then would be their portion?

28 Jesus speaks as the King again. He points forward to His coming again, at the "rebirth," the making all things new. He will be on His throne ruling over the "new world" for which the Jews were looking. His disciples will reign with Him in places of responsibility.

29 Every believer today who leaves anything for the sake of Christ will have great reward. Salvation is not the reward. Our salvation is the free gift of God through Faith in Christ. But our service of discipleship will be rewarded, a hundred times over!

30 Those who may seem least likely to be rewarded will get a greater reward. All of our suffering or loss for the King's sake will be worth it all! 2 Timothy 2.11-13; 1 Peter 4.13.

Chapter 20

The Servants of the King

Parable of the Vineyard Workers, 20.1-16

The King now gives us another parable of the kingdom of heaven. This one gives a call to action by the King. It can be applied in two ways:

1. The Good News Call to Sinners: (1) Their place, in the marketplace of sin. That's where Satan's agents are busy recruiting slaves of sin and shame. Also they are outside the vineyard, the estate of God, lost in sin. (2) Their call. The Good News is God's invitation to salvation. Some are called early in life and can serve the Lord for a whole lifetime, as Samuel, 1 Samuel 3. Others are called in young adulthood, as Saul of Tarsus, Acts 7.58; 9.1-6. And some are reached in old age, when life's day is nearly spent, as Nicodemus, born again when old, John 3.4. But all, young or old, receive the same blessing—Salvation full and free. Good News time is today, 2 Corinthians 6.2.

2. But the main application is to Service of Believers in the Kingdom of Heaven. There are three main parables regarding Service. They are each different and should not be confused. Refer to Chart.

In this one, note the titles of our Lord, verses 1,8,11. He is the Landowner or Master of the House, and Owner of the vineyard. The household suggests a place of family service. The vineyard suggests a place of fruit-producing. He is Lord of it all. As Owner He has complete control, all authority. His will is to invite workers to take part in the harvest.

1-7 So five times the Owner went out to call workers. Early in the morning some came. Then others at mid-morning, noon, mid-afternoon, then finally only one hour before sunset. So the day's work was finished.

8,9 Then they were all paid—the last first and the first last, v.16 and chapter 19.30. They all received one day's wages.

10-12 The full-day workers complained to the Owner that they did not get more than the one-hour workers.

Matthew, presenting Jesus the King

Three Parables on Service

Reference	Item	Opportunity	Ability	Response - Energy	Basis of Reward	Reward or Loss
Matthew 20. 1-16 Vineyard Workers	work: 12 hrs. 9 hrs. 6 hrs. 3 hrs. 1 hr.	various	same	12 hrs. 9 hrs. 6 hrs. 3 hrs. 1 hr.	faithfulness	all received equal pay
Matthew 25. 15-30 talents ($1000 each)	do business with: 5 talents 2 talents 1 talent	various	various	gain: various 100% 100% 0%	faithfulness	rule over many rule over many lost talent
Luke 19.11-27 10 Minas 1= about 3 months' wages	Do business with: 1 mina each	equal	various	gain: various 10=900% 5=400% 0= 0%	faithfulness	rule 10 cities rule 5 cities talent lost

13-15 The Owner reminded them that they received the wage they had agreed to work for. Then He stated two great principles: (1) Sovereignty, or the right to do His own will. The Owner was just and upright—He paid full-day wages. He is never dishonest or unjust, He does not shortchange anyone, He keeps His word. But He also is (2) Gracious, kind, generous. He chose to give the part-time workers the full-day wage (Deuteronomy 24.14,15).

The first who were called had a definite agreement, v.2. The rest were on a "faith by grace" basis. This might suggest the first speak of the nation of Israel, they were under law (agreement). But all the others might speak of Gentiles who are saved by grace not by keeping the law. All benefit from God's sovereign Grace. At best every servant must admit—we are unprofitable servants, Luke 17.10.

There is difference in opportunity for service. Some are called and serve from early morning to evening, as Timothy, 2 Timothy 3.15. But some are "short-time" servants, only mentioned once in the Bible, but who performed good service to God:

Jonathan's armorbearer, 1 Samuel 14.1-15. What did he do?
A nameless woman in 2 Samuel 17.19. What did she do?

Ananias, in Acts 9.10-19. What did he do?
Prince Seraiah, Jeremiah 51.59-64. What was he told to do?
All these were faithful so received full reward. Let us do faithfully whatever He gives us to do.

Shadows Again, 20.17-19

Again the King draws His disciples aside. They are on their way up to Jerusalem. He reminds them again of what will happen there. He had done so in chapters 16 and 17 but they still needed reminding. Once more He uses those awful words: betrayed (handed over), condemned to death, made fun of, whipped, nailed to a cross, and raised to life. But this time He adds the Gentiles and crucified, nailed to a cross.

Selfish Honor-Seeking, 20.20-28

20,21 This almost seems like an interruption. Mrs. Zebedee comes to Jesus to ask a favor. She wants her two sons, James and John, to sit on the right and left hand of the King! That would be the highest honors of the kingdom. No matter about the Savior's cross and sufferings, they wanted the crowns.

22,23 But that would be reserved for those who drank deepest from the cup of suffering for Christ. God the Father will appoint those honors. The boast of James and John in verse 22 almost sounds as proud as Peter's boast in chapter 26.33-35. Eventually James did drink of the cup of death for the Lord's sake, Acts 12.1,2. And John also did after a long life of service.

24 The other ten disciples were angry with James and John for wanting the highest places. This was probably because they themselves wanted it.

25-27 In any case they **all** needed another lesson in humility. How patiently the King deals with His followers! He reminded them that earthly rulers put their important people up high. But His kingdom is just the opposite. The way up is down; the way down is up. True greatness is becoming the lowly servant-slave of others. One who tries to get the high place will surely be brought low, 23.11,12.

28 And of course, our greatest example is our King Himself. He stooped so low when He came to earth, not to be served but to do the serving. Love **always** serves and gives. He gave His life for all, 2 Corinthians 5.14; Hebrews 2.9, but as many as receive Him benefit from it, John 1.12.

> Would you be chief? Then servant be.
> Would you go up? Go down!
> But go as low as ever you will—
> The Highest One has been lower still!
> Praise His Name!

Sight, 20.29-34

A large crowd was following Jesus as He left Jericho on the road to Jerusalem. Two blind men called to Him for mercy. They were like two other blind men in chapter 9.27-31. (See notes on that story.) The nation of Israel rejected their Messiah-Deliverer. They "saw" physically but were blind to Him spiritually. These two physically blind men "saw" Him spiritually and were blessed. The seeing ones were made blind and the blind were made to see. Read our Lord's words about this in John 9.39-41.

These two men are pictures of all of us in our spiritual need:

1. The Condition of the Sinner —blind, in darkness, Romans 1.21; Ephesians 4.18
2. The Cry for Mercy —pointed to the right Person: Lord, Son of David
    —persistent: not giving up, v.31
    —personal: have mercy on us
3. The Compassion (Pity) of the Savior, vs. 32-34
    —interested in the needy
    —inquires for Faith: what do you want?
    —important request: for sight
    —immediate response: He touched them
4. The Consequence (Results) — instantly healed
    —deliverance from darkness to light
    —discipleship: they followed Him.

Has this wonderful King healed your blindness? Are you following Him—walking in the light? 1 John 1.7.

Chapter 21

The King Enters the Holy City

The King's Official Entry Into Jerusalem, 21.1-11

1-8 1. Preparation. At last the King drew near the City of the King, which is Jerusalem. Forerunners are sent ahead to make preparations. The animals, a donkey and her colt, are obtained and prepared, v.7. The roadway is prepared, covered with clothes and small olive branches. It looks as if there will be a big parade.

2. Explanation. But first Matthew gives us another "identity picture" from the Old Testament. Zechariah 9.9 foretold that Israel's King would come. He is the Righteous One having Salvation. What special royal sign would be shown? Usually a king comes with majesty and pomp. But this King would be gentle and humble: (1) Instead of royal expensive robes He would be dressed in home-made garments; (2) Instead of riding on a beautiful, high-bred horse, He comes riding on a lowly donkey, the beast of burden; (3) Instead of noblemen, statesmen and military leaders coming with him, His close attendants are humble fishermen; (4) Instead of conquering armies He is followed by peasants from Galilee. What humble grace this King shows!

3. Exaltation. And yet He is praised and honored. Large crowds shout, *Hosanna, save us. O Son of David. Blessed is He who comes in the name of the Lord.* And it is all connected with heaven. *In the highest.* Angels used that word in Luke 2.14 when the King was born. Find three times in Luke 1 where He is called Highest or Most High. See Psalm 118.24-27.

10,11 The whole city was stirred, shaken as by an earthquake. Everyone asked: Who is this? Was the answer: King of Kings and Lord of Lords? No, not yet. He is King and Lord and in a future day will be recognized by all. But now He receives praise as the lowly Jesus of Nazareth in Galilee.

Then why did He make this public display? To fulfil Zechariah 9. He was officially presenting Himself to Israel, giving them this final challenge to receive and welcome Him, their true Messiah. He comes to His own, John 1.11. Will they receive Him? Have you?

For the interested reader here is a brief outline of how the donkey here pictures the sinner:

(1) Tied, in bondage to sin, John 8.32-34;
(2) Unbroken, never ridden, Luke 19.30,—self-will, John 5.40;
(3) Unclean animal, defilement of sin, Leviticus 11.3,4;
(4) Under the curse, Exodus 13.13, unless redeemed by a lamb, John 1.29; 1 Peter 1.18; but
(5) Loosed, freed, v.33; John 8.36;
(6) Brought to Jesus, John 1.41,42;
(7) Submissive to His will, v.6;
(8) Honored to bear Jesus to the city (world)—our privilege.

The King in the Temple, 21.12-16

Where would you think a king would go first in his own royal city? To his palace? Probably an earthly king would. Our King had no palace in Jerusalem. (But He will "visit" three palaces there, in chapter 26.3,57; Luke 23.6-12; John 18.28. Look up and write down whose palaces these were. Jesus did not enter those palaces to reside or rule or rest. He was on trial for His life!)

Instead the King went directly to the temple. In the Old Testament this represented God's presence with His people, 2 Chronicles 6.18 and 7.1,2. He met with them there and they worshiped Him.

But all that had changed. Israel had turned away from their true God. They had gone after idols, false gods. So the Lord had left His temple empty, Ezekiel 10.4,18,19; 11.23. He sent Israel away into captivity. Now, in New Testament times some of Israel had returned to the land but only a few were true followers of the Lord.

Now the King enters the temple and what does He find? People were buying and selling sacrificial animals and birds, wine, salt and oil. These were all necessary things for sacrifices but it was the wrong place to be doing the business. Money changers were those who would exchange Roman and foreign money for the temple half-shekel tax. (In doing this they made a profit too!). They had all defiled God's holy temple making it a den of thieves. See Isaiah 56.7; Jeremiah 7.11. They changed God's house to a robber's den, prayer to thievery, worship of God to worship of riches, glorifying God to grasping gold.

14,15 But the King cleared out all the wrong-doers. There was a brief restoration to its original beauty. The needy, blind and lame came to Him in the temple and He healed them. Children shouted and sang His praises. It was a lovely scene of blessing and praise. This is a little picture of what believers' lives should be like. 1 Corinthians 6.19,20 says that we are God's temple. As He lives in us He can pour out blessing to others. This will result in praise to His name. But we must be kept clean from sin and defilement.

15,16 These verses give us the official reaction of the priests and teachers: Rejection! They saw the wonderful things and heard wonderful praises and they were angry! They should have joined in praising God. But their hearts were far from God. Angrily they challenge Jesus to stop the children's praises. But He quotes Psalm 8.2, another "identity picture." This Psalm pointed to Himself, the Messiah. He is glorified even today by children's praises.

17 Sad result: He left them, priests and teachers; He left the temple, their temple, not God's; He left the city—increasing in rebellion. He will not stay where He is not wanted. But He was welcome in Bethany. Is He welcome in your heart?

The Fig Tree, 21.18-22

In the Old Testament the vineyard and the fig tree were used as pictures of Israel, as Joel 1.7; 1 Kings 4.25; compare Luke 13.6.

18,19 Early on this morning the King walked from Bethany back to Jerusalem. Alongside the road was a fig tree. How delicious and refreshing some nice ripe figs would be to a person hot and hungry from the journey! He went to pick some figs but found only leaves. (Mark 11.13 says it was not the season for ripe figs yet. But in Isaiah 28.4 and Hosea 9.10 we read about some early trees which have ripe fruit before leaves.) The Lord cursed this tree and it began to wither at once. This was unusual for Jesus who always blessed, healed and helped. This is the only miracle of pure judgment He performed. Judgment is His "strange work," Isaiah 28.21.

It is all a picture or symbol of Israel as a nation. Their unbelief caused them to reject their Messiah-King. Their rejection brought judgment, when Jerusalem was destroyed in A.D. 70. The difference is that, while the fig tree died, Israel will be restored or resurrected in a future day of blessing. See Romans 11.

20-22 Faith will bring blessings. Even small faith in GOD can bring big results, chapter 17.20, 1 Corinthians 13.2. Our mountain of sin or need of any kind can be removed by our God in whom we trust, if our faith is complete and genuine.

The King Challenged Again, 21.23-27

Jesus returned to the temple to teach the people. Now the chief priests and elders demanded, Who gave you the right to do this? He replied with another question, What right did John the Baptizer have for his preaching and teaching?

They knew John's message was from God but they didn't want to admit it. They would like to say it was only human, but they feared that the people would rise up against them. So the easy way out was: We don't know. So Jesus refused to answer their question, not because He didn't know but because of their unbelief. Instead He began telling them three parable-stories.

The Parable of the Two Sons, 21.28-32

A father wanted his two sons to work in his vineyard. The first refused to go but later changed his mind (repented) and obeyed. The second promised to go but never did. Jesus asked those chief priests and elders, Which son did the father's will? Naturally they answered, The first one. Then Jesus made His important point: You have never believed and repented. But the hated and despised tax collectors and immoral people did repent. By their faith they enter the kingdom of God ahead of you!

Parable of the Vineyard, 21.33-46

Again the King gave them a story-picture. Like a Master Artist He used a few brief sentences to sketch a picture they could easily understand.

33-36 He used the picture that Isaiah used in chapter 5.1-7. A vineyard was prepared, planted and protected. Its purpose was to produce fruit for the owner who rented it to tenants. At harvest time he sent servants to collect his fruit. Do you see the picture? The vineyard is Israel. The rulers and leaders were the responsible tenants. Responsibility is the key word. The Owner is the Lord who sent the Old Testament prophets. But Israel rejected, beat and killed them. See 2 Chronicles 24.21; 36.16; Nehemiah 9.26 as examples.

37-39 Finally the Owner sent His own dear Son, Mark 12.6. But they threw Him out and killed Him. See chapter 26.3-4.

40 Now Jesus forces the chief priests and rulers to pass judgment on themselves. What ought to be done to those tenants?

41 He has so forcefully and clearly drawn the picture that they must pass severe judgment on the tenants: Put them to death and rent the vineyard to others who will produce fruit for the Owner. And they were exactly right!

42,43 Then Jesus quoted Psalm 118.22,23, another "identity picture." The Stone or Rock is our Lord Himself. They themselves are the tenants and will be judged. Others, Gentiles, will be blessed. Israel was rejecting the capstone and the building, temple, would never be complete without Him.

44 Now the very solemn warning: Jesus is like a stumbling-stone to the pride of unbelief. If we are broken by it we can be blessed. That means if our pride and unbelief are broken down to humble faith in Christ we can be saved. But if we refuse this we can only expect to be crushed in judgment. See Daniel 2.40,45; Isaiah 60.12.

So the King has drawn out a number of confessions by the chief priests and rulers as to their own: (1) lack of honesty, v.27; (2) lack of fitness to rule, v.27; (3) lack of repentance, vs.29,32; (4) responsibility for His death, v.41; and (5) resulting judgment, v.44.

45,46 They knew all this was true. But how did they respond? Did they repent and confess their sins and ask for mercy and forgiveness? Not at all. They only hardened their hearts, and looked for some way to arrest Him. How sad!

Chapter 22

The King and Leaders of Israel

Parable of the Wedding Feast, 22.1-14

In chapter 21 the King has spoken of responsibility. Now in this parable we find privilege. The king represents God as He prepares a wedding feast for His Son, our Lord Jesus Christ. It is a great privilege, or honor, to be a guest at such a feast. We notice there are three invitations here.

3   *First Invitation* — to those already invited before. As in Esther 5.8; 6.14, the message is sent: Come, the time for the feast is here. This group would represent the nation Israel. They had been given all the Old Testament prophecies and were instructed in God's plans. Now, through our Lord and His disciples, they were being invited to come, by faith in Christ, to partake of the royal feast. But Israel refused to come. This would represent the 3½ years of Christ's public ministry.

4-7   *Second invitation* — the feast is now ready. This suggests the Calvary work of our Savior, "It is finished." After the death and resurrection of our Lord the next phase of the invitation goes out through the book of Acts. First the Jews then the Gentiles are invited. A few believed and obeyed the message. But mostly the response was: (1) Indifference, careless self-centered living. Many went about their own affairs—to their farms or business, not caring about the king or his son; (2) Others hated the king and they beat and killed his servants. Examples of this are in Acts 7.54-60, Stephen; and Acts 12.1-4, James. But the King sent armies and destroyed Jerusalem in A.D. 70.

8-10   *Third Invitation* — covers the present time. The Good News is God's invitation to Salvation. It is being preached around the world to Jews and Gentiles. The "go" in verse 9 represents the "go" in chapter 28.19. Everyone, good or bad (in the Jew's eyes) is invited. "Whosoever will" applies to religious Jews like Saul, Acts 9, and to hardened Gentiles like the Philippian Jailer in Acts 16.

11-13 But another warning is given. No one is allowed at this feast without proper wedding clothes. (Jews should remember the words of Zephaniah 1.7,8.) The wedding clothes speak of holiness and righteousness we all need if we are to see God, Hebrews 12.14. They picture the Garments of Salvation referred to in the following verses: Isaiah 61.10; Luke 15.22; 1 Corinthians 1.30; Genesis 3.21.

Anyone not "in Christ" will be left outside the banquet halls of heaven, verse 13. See Revelation 21.27 and 22.14,15.

14 The Lord ends this parable with "many are invited" which refers to the "whosoever will" group. But only a few respond, and they are "choice" or "special" to God. The word applies to Christ Himself in 1 Peter 2.6. He is the Chief One, the Choice One, the Precious One. And the same word is applied to believers, 1 Peter 1.2; 2.4,9. Look up these verses and worship the God of your salvation. What wonderful privilege believers are brought into!

Next Matthew presents four test questions. Three different groups come to Jesus with questions. Notice how He answers them.

First Test Question: Paying Taxes, 22.15-22

15 First the Pharisees join with Herodians to try to lay a trap for the King. Herodians were a political party, and Pharisees were a religious party. It is interesting to see how enemies of the Lord could join together with others whom they themselves hated in an effort to catch and destroy Jesus.

16,17 They come to Him to ask a question. This could be called a **Political** attack. 1) The **Purpose**—to trap Him into saying something wrong. 2) The **Plan**—to use flattery to throw Him off guard. Notice this in verse 16—they didn't really mean it or they would have had to believe Him and accept His teachings. 3) The **Problem** stated—Is it right to pay the poll-tax to Caesar? This tax was to be paid by all males 14 years old and over, and all females over 12, up to the age of 65. 4) The **Plot**—if He answered "Yes" they would tell all the Jews that He was not a true, loyal Jew. They hated the Romans and hated paying taxes to them. If He answered "No" they would report Him to the Romans as a rebel or revolutionary. He would then be arrested and punished.

18,19 But notice the perfect wisdom of the King. He knew their evil intentions—He could read their thoughts (He is God!). He asked them to show Him a coin (He was so poor He didn't have one).

20,22 He asked them whose face and name were on the coin and they answered, Caesar's. Then He stated a great law of His own Kingdom: (1) Give to government what is due to government.

We are to obey the laws, respect and honor authority, and pay taxes. All true followers of the Great King will always do this. Read Romans 13.1-7; 1 Peter 2.13,14; Matthew 17.24-27. Are you doing this?

(2) But we must not stop there. We also are to give to God what belongs to Him. Here are some things we should give to God (look up and fill in).

Psalm 29.2 _____

Psalm 56.12 _____

Psalm 96.7 _____

Matthew 2.11 _____

Romans 12.1 _____

Can you add more references?

His enemies were amazed at His wisdom but they left Him and went away. Isn't that sad? Why did they go away?

Second Test Question: Resurrection, 22.23-33

23 Now the Sadducees take their turn. These people were rationalists, that is, they did not believe in resurrection or in spirits, verse 23, and Acts 23.8.

24-28 Their challenge: (1) they quoted from Moses, Deuteronomy 25.5. (2) they told a story (probably made up?) — seven brothers all having one and the same wife; all died childless and then the woman died. Their question: whose wife will she be in a resurrection? In this way they were mocking the idea of resurrection.

29 The King told them they were wrong for two reasons: (1) They did not know their Old Testament Bible. See Job 19.25-27 and Psalm 16.9-11. (2) They did not know God's power. See Genesis 22.5; 2 Kings 4.35; Isaiah 26.19. God does not want us to be ignorant of these things.

30 About Resurrection—life beyond death is not going to be like the present life on earth. Heaven is another, new life—not this life on earth repeated.

31,32 About the Scriptures—He quoted from Exodus 3.6. God said I **AM** (present tense) and not I **was**—(in the past) the God of Abraham, Isaac and Jacob. These men died many years before but they still were alive to God, Luke 20.38. The Sadducees were wrong—there IS life after death. For believers in Christ it is a life of bliss and deep happiness, John 14.19; Philippians 1.23. But for unbelievers it is one of weeping, wailing and pain, verse 13; Luke 16.24. Which will it be for you?

Matthew 22.23-45

33 Crowds were listening. They were amazed at His teaching but that was all.

Third Test Question: Which Commandment? 22.34-40

34 The Pharisees heard how the Lord had silenced and defeated the Sadducees. So they got together to make another attack—this time a **Legal** one.

35,36 One of them was a teacher of the law. The Law of Moses contained 613 precepts or direct orders, from Exodus to Deuteronomy. These had been summarized in the Ten Commandments, Exodus 20. This lawyer asked Jesus to state which one was the greatest commandment. In other words, it might be hard to remember and keep 613 commands but which one could we keep which would cover them all?

37,38 The Royal answer was: Love God perfectly. The King went outside the Ten Commandments and quoted from Deuteronomy 6.5: Love God with all your being: Heart—the will; Soul—the affections; Mind—the understanding; Strength—the body.

39 But the King added a second one: Love your neighbor as yourself. This is found in Leviticus 19.18. This always must go with the first. It is the outward proof of obeying the first, 1 John 4.20.

40 All the requirements of God's Law are fulfilled by LOVE, Romans 13.10. If we love God perfectly everything in our lives will fit into its proper place. But **who** can do that? Only the Perfect Man (our Lord Jesus) perfectly fulfilled the Law. What about all the rest of us? We are sinners and need a Savior. And, praise God, Christ is the Savior of sinners; He came to save us and make us fit for heaven, 2 Corinthians 5.21; Galatians 3.10-14.

Fourth Test Question: Who? 22.41-46.

41,42 Then, while the Pharisees were still standing there, the King "turned the tables around." He asked **them** the final test question. This was two questions in one. They professed to be looking for the coming Messiah-Deliverer. So He asked for their opinion: Whose Son is He? At once they replied correctly, the Son of David. That was according to such verses as Isaiah 9.6,7; 11.1-3.

43,44 Then Jesus quoted from Psalm 110.1 which was written by David as guided by the Holy Spirit (as were all Old Testament writers, 2 Timothy 3.16; 2 Peter 1.20,21). David wrote about the Lord-Jehovah speaking to the Messiah whom David called "my Lord."

45 If David called Him "Lord" how could He be David's son? The answer is that Jesus was both Son of God (His deity) **and** Son of

Man or Son of David (His humanity). He was the God-Man. But the Pharisees absolutely refused to believe that truth, so they could not answer the Lord's question. They completely failed the test.

By faith we can rejoice in this lovely revelation of the true glories of our Lord Jesus Christ. Psalm 110.1 is so important it is quoted four times in the New Testament: here in verse 44; Acts 2.34,35; Hebrews 1.13; Hebrews 10.13. They tell of His exaltation, victory and Deity.

46 His enemies are silenced. None will dare debate with Him again. But Satan has another method of attack, see chapter 26.

Chapter 23

The King and Leaders of Israel (cont'd)

We understand from chapter 24.1 that the King was in the temple as He spoke these words in chapter 23. Here we have the King's final message to Israel. It probably was on the day before His arrest. He was only hours away from Calvary.

The so-called Sermon on the Mount, chapter 5 to 7, was the start of His public preaching while chapter 23 is the end. In the first He spoke of nine sweet "blesseds," in the last eight terrible woes. In both He spoke several times of hypocrites; of the wrong use of oaths; of long prayers and the wrong of doing things to show off before men. In both He referred to the Old Testament Scriptures.

Description of Israel's Leaders, 23.1-7

1,2 The Seat of Moses represented the authority of the Law of Moses. We are told there was a chair at the front of the synagogue where the senior Jewish teacher would sit when instructing the Jews. When he spoke from that chair he represented God, Leviticus 10.11; Malachi 2.7. The people must obey and do what he said, Deuteronomy 17.8-13.

3 But here the King said that the teachers and Pharisees did not practise what they preached. So He told the people to do what they said (the Law of Moses) but not what they **did**. It is not right to teach truth but not live according to that truth, Romans 2.19-24.

4 They kept adding their own rules and regulations which made heavy loads which the people could not bear. The teachers themselves made no effort to help them either. See Acts 15.10.

5 Today we call them "show-offs." They do everything so **men** will see them. This is Pride. They read Exodus 13.9 and Deuteronomy

6.8,9 and literally made little boxes to fasten on the forehead and left hand. Inside was a parchment on which was written four portions of the Law: Exodus 13.3-10 and 11-16; Deuteronomy 6.5-9 and 11.13-21. They considered these as "charms." Some would make their boxes larger than others so they would look more "religious." But they didn't put God's Word in their **hearts** and obey it, Psalm 119.11.

In Numbers 15.38,39 the Jews were commanded to wear a hem or tassle of blue on their coats. This was to remind them to obey God's Word. But again these leaders were proudly making bigger tassles "to be seen of men"—to look more "religious" than the others.

6,7 They loved the honor-seats at feasts and the important seats in their church. Why? Because of their pride. They loved popularity and the title, Rabbi or Teacher. It was "ME first." So the leaders were described as having proud walk and empty talk.

Disciples Described, 23.8-12

Now the King tells His followers they are to be different. True disciples of the King are all brothers, v. 8; sons of one Father, v.9; learners, v.10; servants, v.11; humble, v.12.

They are not to take titles such as Teacher, Leader or Father. Now, of course, in human life we all have human teachers and fathers. And in the church we have leaders. We should honor all such. But we are not to take official titles of position. Nowhere in the entire New Testament is any believer given the title Reverend, or Father, or Master (Teacher). All glory and honor goes to Christ alone.

11,12 The King again emphasizes what true greatness is: lowly service. Remember how He taught this in chapter 20.25-28. He Himself is the great Example.

Eight Woes, 23.13-32

Now the King turns to the leaders of Israel. He utters some of His most solemn warnings. Seven times His righteous anger flashes against the hypocrisy of these false-hearted men as He points out their faults and sins. Eight times He uses the words, Woe to you, meaning, Alas, how terrible for you. In these words we see righteousness mingled with love, anger blended with gentleness, law with grace. The Woes are really wails of compassion, as we shall see shortly.

13 In unbelief they would not enter the kingdom of heaven themselves. But worse, they were hindering others who wanted to enter. For examples of this see John 9.22 and 12.42. Also Matthew 18.6,7.

Matthew 23.6-24

14 (This verse is omitted in some old Bibles, but it is found in Mark 12.40 and Luke 20.47.) These hypocrites made long prayers for a show on the Sabbaths and holy days. Hidden underneath is that they robbed poor widows of money and homes during the week. (If she couldn't pay the rent they would heartlessly put her out of the house onto the street!) They were also known to cheat wealthy widows out of their money (in the name of religion, of course). They tried to cover up by their show of long prayers. (This probably refers to "the 18 prayers" which were regular devotions for Pharisees.) But because they did all this in the name of "religion" their judgment would be all the greater.

15 They delighted in making converts to their own party, especially when they could gain money in doing so. But such people were converted to an empty religion. They were twice as bad as the Pharisees because the bad habits of the Pharisees were added to their own bad habits of heathen life. So they were in a sad state.

16-22 Blind guides can only lead blind people into the pit, Luke 6.39.

They had turned away from the Light of the world (John 8.12) and the Truth (John 14.6). There only remained blindness and darkness. They saw the gold in the temple and valued it more than the temple itself or rather the God of the temple. It was gold more than God. So the King corrected their wrong teaching about swearing and oaths. Do you remember what He said in chapter 5.34,35?

23,24 Tithing, or giving a tenth, to the Lord was part of the Law of Moses. In general it included crops and vegetables, Leviticus 27.30, Deuteronomy 14.22,23.

Tithing of herbs and spices was added by the old teachers as an addition to the Law. It was approved by our Lord in verse 23, but He found fault with their attitude. The mint and dill (anise) and cummin were common, small herbs, plentiful and cheap. (Mint was used to cover the floor of some synagogues to fill the room with nice fragrance.) The Pharisees were proudly taking great care to tithe these cheap herbs from their gardens, but they totally neglected the very important requirements of the Law: justice—doing the right things; mercy—showing kindness and forgiveness; and good faith or honesty—not cheating.

Verse 14 has already given us an example of this. Saying a lot of long, empty prayers and giving a tenth of some little sprigs of mint, — how does this compare with robbing widows and cheating neighbors? God looks at our hearts and motives. He will not let a little mint blind His eyes to murder, theft and adultery. See Micah 6.8; Hosea 6.6; 12.6; Matthew 9.13; 12.7.

24 Here He illustrates this. They were straining a gnat (a very small fly) out of their wine but swallowing a camel. The gnat and the camel were probably the smallest and largest living creatures they would know about in those days. The Old Testament forbad their eating either one, Leviticus 11.23,42, 44. Their sense of values was all out of balance. They were making a big mountain out of a little pile of sand and were shutting their eyes to what God called important matters.

25-28 The next two Woes can be called, "Outside and Inside."
(1) Dirty dishes; they carefully washed the outside so people thought they were clean people. But the King saw the inside: greed and sin. (2) Tombs, where dead people were buried. Every year the Jews carefully whitewashed the tombs, on the 15th day of Adar (our February-March). Tombs and graves were ritually unclean, Numbers 19.16. So they were whitewashed to warn people away from touching them. The whitewash (made from chalk) would easily wash off in the rain. But even though the outside was white the inside was unchanged—full of corpses and bones. Psalm 5.9; Romans 3.13. This all reminds us that man looks on the outside but God looks on the heart, 1 Samuel 16.7. Our hearts need to be cleaned by the precious blood of Christ, 1 John 1.7-9.

29-32 The present and the past. "We are better than our ancestors," they said. They pretended to honor the old prophet-martyrs by making beautiful tombs and memorials for them. But the King said that they were true sons of their wicked forefathers. This would be proved shortly when they murdered the King Himself. See 21.33-44.

Summary and Final Warning, 23.33-36

33,34 John the Baptizer had asked, Who has warned you? Now the King asks, How will you escape judgment? It would be impossible because they had refused to listen to warnings. More prophets and messengers are going to be sent (as in the book of Acts) but Israel would reject, whip, chase and kill them. See chapter 22.6 notes.

35,36 The terrible result would be—multiplied guilt. All of the innocent blood shed throughout the Old Testament was not Israel's direct crime. For example, Abel was killed by Cain 2500 years before Israel became a nation. But the murder of Abel was the first of a long battle line between right and wrong, between God and His enemies. Zechariah was the last recorded murder in the Old Testament, 2 Chronicles 24.21. (In the old Hebrew Bible 2 Chronicles was the last book. So the Lord is simply talking here about the "whole Old Testament" from beginning to end, from Genesis to Chronicles.) The nation of Israel was very often guilty of rebelling against God. Now in a day or two they were going to murder their Messiah-King. That would be the climax of their whole wicked history. (Peter presses this charge against them in Acts 2.23,36-40; 4.10. Stephen did so in Acts 7.)

35 There is a difficulty regarding Zechariah. Some think he refers to the son of Jehoiada in 2 Chronicles 24.20. Matthew calls this Zechariah the son of Berakiah or Baruch. Luke 11.51 omits the father's name. Others quote from an Old Jewish writing called the Targum, which says that Zechariah the prophet, son of Iddo, was murdered in the Sanctuary (temple). This is not recorded in the Bible but it may be true history. So we cannot be certain about this.

Sad Farewell, 23.37-39

Now the words flow with tears. The great loving heart of God overflows through the words of His beloved Son. Where else can we find deeper feeling of strong love and compassion? Jerusalem, beloved city of God, yet how very guilty—killing and stoning God's messengers. Israel's guilt was only exceeded by the grace and love which longed to save her. Where sin increased God's wonderful grace increased more yet, Romans 5.20.

Listen to the heart-throb of almighty love: How often I longed and earnestly wanted to save you. Notice the picture He used: the hen calling and gathering her little chicks to safety and shelter from the enemy, under her wings. It is a lovely picture, used often in the Old Testament. Look up Deuteronomy 32.11; Psalm 17.8; 36.7; 57.1; 61.4; Isaiah 31.5; Malachi 4.2. The believer rejoices in the warmth and strength of God's tender love and care—under His wings!

But how sad was Israel's response—she refused, she WOULD NOT. God's loving willingness was blocked by man's stubborn **unwillingness**. And God let Israel have her way!

38 The result was their house was left empty and forsaken, Jeremiah 12.7; 22.5. This refers to (1) the temple, abandoned by God and destroyed in A.D. 70. (2) the nation itself, scattered, chased and hated by enemies ever since. The King was departing from the temple and from the nation, see Ezekiel 10.4,18,19.

39 They will not see Him again, UNTIL. In the future there will again be blessing for Israel. This is linked with their national repentance at the King's coming again. See Deuteronomy 4.29-31, Hosea 3.4,5; Zechariah 12.10; 14.8-11.

And now in the next two chapters the King will focus the attention of His disciples on future events.

Chapter 24

The King Foretells Future Events

1   Jesus left the temple for the last time, chapter 23.38. The disciples called His attention to the beauty and size of their great temple. Old writings tell us that is was built of very large stones, some 50 to 60 feet long (15-20 meters). Beautiful white marble pillars were up to 40 feet (13 meters) high.

2   But He said something which must have shocked them: That beautiful temple was going to be totally destroyed—not one stone left on another.

3   A short time later as Jesus was sitting on the Mount of Olives, His troubled disciples came to ask Him more about these things. Notice there are really two questions here, and the King's answer is the longest one He ever gave—it covers almost two chapters.

There are different explanations of these prophecies. Some think the whole message was fulfilled at the destruction of Jerusalem in A.D.70. But this really could not be. There are some details which can apply to that event, but they can apply to other times in history too. We will here suggest the simplest outline we can without getting into all the details. *See Footnote,

---

*Footnote: For those interested in deeper study of this most interesting subject of Prophecy we suggest you read *God's Timetable* by D.B. Long, and *What Next? a Primer on Prophecy* by R.E. Harlow. Both published by Everyday Publications Inc.

Matthew 24.1-28

Two Questions

(1) When will **this** happen? That is, what Jesus was talking about in verse 2, the temple destroyed. Matthew 24, Mark 13 and Luke 21 all record this message, called the Olivet Prophecy. But there are some differences. We believe Matthew and Mark omit the specific answer to this first question. Luke 21.20-24 specially mentions the destruction of Jerusalem (including the temple) by the armies (of Rome). This was literally fulfilled in the year A.D. 70 when Roman armies destroyed and burned the whole place. One old historian wrote that they dug and buried everything so that it looked as if no one had ever lived there. Some parts of Matthew 24 could be applied to that awful time, but not all. We believe they really belong to the answer of Question Two. (2) What will be the sign or signal of your Coming and of the End of the Age (not end of the world, as in some Bibles)? The Jews including the disciples thought of two ages: (1) this age, the then-present time of waiting for the coming of Messiah, and (2) the age to come, the setting up of Messiah's kingdom.

The Signs, 24.4-31

This whole section refers to the period just before the "end of the age." We will just point out **key** words which pin-point events.

4-8 General conditions are described: false Christs, deceivers, wars and fighting, famines and earthquakes. But the **end** is not yet—it is only the beginning of birthpain sorrows. We suggest this refers to the first half of the seven years of Tribulation.

9-14 Reference to this time continues. Note "then," v. 9 and "at that time," v.10. Israel will be persecuted, arrested, put to death, hated by all nations. There will be more false prophets and increased wickedness. Only true believers will remain true to the end and be saved. The Good News of the Kingdom will be preached to the whole world by a faithful few, the believing Jews, Revelation 14.6,7. Then the end will come, v.14, that is, the end of the first half of the Tribulation, the beginning of sorrows.

15-28 Note the When, v.15; Then, vs. 16,21; At that time, v.23. All refer to the same moment in verse 15. The Sign is the Abomination, the horrible thing referred to by Daniel, 9.27; 11.31; 12.11. See also 2 Thessalonians 2.3,4. This is the Sign the King referred to. The Great Tribulation or Great Distress, of 3½ years, or 42 months, or 1260 days, is referred to in many Scriptures, as Daniel 12.7; Revelation 11.2,3; 12.6. The faithful are advised to run away, hurry, pray, don't listen to false prophets, reject false Messiahs. Brief, awful descriptions of those days are: dreadful, most terrible in all history, shortened in order that God's chosen people may survive, many dead bodies and vultures.

138   Matthew, presenting Jesus the King

29 Right at the end of that period come the terrors of this verse. Sun, moon, stars and heavenly bodies all shaken and changed. We believe these will be literal, actual physical changes which everyone will see. But it also can refer to symbolic changes in the ranks of men's authorities and governments. Whole nations will be shaken in fear and perplexity, Luke 21.

30 Right at that time the King Himself will come on the clouds with power and great glory, Daniel 7.13,14. When HIS Sign is seen in the sky all nations of earth will weep and wring their hands and faint in terror, Luke 21.25-27; Revelation 1.7.

31 His armies are angels. They will obey the loud trumpet call and spread out over the whole earth to gather the King's true followers to Himself, Deuteronomy 30.4,5. What joy for them after all the awful suffering they had just gone through!

This ends the King's direct answer to question #2. But He has more to say about the subject in illustrations, exhortations and parables.

The Fig Tree, 24.32-35

Here is a lesson for all. The fig tree (and all trees, Luke 21) by their buds and leaves show signs of Springtime. When we see them we know Summer is near. So the people of God can know the coming of the King is very near when the signs given in verses 4-28 are seen.

34 "This generation" may mean the Jews as a race. In spite of all the persecution there will be Israelites on earth when the King comes. Or, "this generation" may refer to the people living at the time the fig tree buds (the forming of the nation Israel) who will live to see the full summertime of Christ's coming in power and glory.

35 Peoples and nations may come and go; heaven and earth itself will pass away, Hebrews 1.10-12. But the Word of the King will remain forever, Psalm 119.89. His authority is solid and eternal. You can depend on what He says!

The Day and Hour Unknown, 24.36-51

Now the King uses some more illustrations about His Coming. These show it will be a surprise. No one knows the day nor the hour it will take place, vs. 36,42,43,44,50.

37-39 The flood in Noah's time, Genesis 6-8. People were busy living their wicked lives—too busy to bother about the warning of coming flood. They lived like this right up to the very day Noah and his family entered the ark. Surprise! They were all destroyed.

40,41 Two field workers and two women grinding at the mill. It is life and work as usual. But suddenly one of each is missing. Surprise! No warning.

42-44 The owner of the house never knows what night the thief may break in. One night—Surprise! He has been robbed.

44 Lesson for all: The coming again of Christ will be a surprise to all except those who are ready and watching for Him. See Acts 16.30,31. If you are not ready that day will take you by surprise and you will be lost.

45-51 Two kinds of servants. The faithful one will keep busy serving the King—feeding, helping, encouraging His people. The Master will come unexpectedly—Surprise! The faithful servant will be rewarded and blessed.

The other servant is called wicked because he didn't believe the Master would return soon. So he got drunk and beat the other servants. The Master comes unannounced. Surprise! The wicked servant is punished with the hypocrites (false professors). So, the message for us all today is in verse 42: Keep watch; Be ready, v.44.

Chapter 25

The King Foretells Future Events (cont'd)

Parable of the Ten Virgins, 25.1-13

1 This story is linked with the Kingdom of Heaven. It tells us of followers of the King who are real and those who are only pretending. It refers us back to chapter 13, and teaches us the importance of being ready for the King's coming, pictured here as the Bridegroom. Ten young ladies went out to meet Him. It was night so they took their lamps with them.

2-4 Five were wise enough to be sure they had oil so their lamps would stay lit. But the other five foolishly had none. Lamps are a picture of witness and testimony, 5.15. But oil is needed as fuel. It is a symbol of the Holy Spirit who lives in every true believer as the Source of life and testimony, John 14.17. But anyone who does not have the Holy Spirit does not belong to Christ and therefore is not saved, Romans 8.9.

So here we see five believers and five unbelievers. They all look alike on the outside—all ten had lamps and all went out to meet the Bridegroom. But the difference was—five were real possessors of salvation, the other five were mere pretenders.

5,6 A long time passed, v.19, which speaks of the Lord's longsuffering, 2 Peter 3.9. They all grew drowsy and fell asleep. Then suddenly, at midnight, they were awakened, "Here's the Bridegroom, come and meet Him" (Another "surprise," see chapter 24). See 1 Thessalonians 4.16; 5.1-10.

7,8 Then the truth came out—the five foolish ones had no oil, no life, no faith. They begged the wise ones to give them some oil. But this was not possible. No one can give his or her salvation to someone else. They were not selfish, but they were not able to help them.

9-12 The foolish ones could only rush to the shops to buy some for themselves, Proverbs 23.23; Isaiah 55.1. But it was too late. The Bridegroom took the wise ones into the wedding feast and the door was closed. The foolish ones ran fast and earnestly pleaded to be let in but they were too late.

Many people intend to get to heaven some day but they keep on listening to Satan's whisper, Wait until tomorrow. But tomorrow never comes. Have you been putting off your salvation?

13 Listen to the King's warning—Keep watching. We don't know what day or hour He will come. So be ready. Trust Him today, 2 Corinthians 6.2.

Parable of the Three Servants, 25.14-30

Not only are we responsible to be ready when our King (Bridegroom) comes, we are also responsible to serve Him well until He comes. That is the lesson of this story.

14 The Man here is our King Himself, Owner of all things. He went on a journey—back to heaven. He had servants on earth and He called them together and gave them each a large sum of money. They were to make use of it for Him. Do you remember from chapter 18 that one "talent" was worth about 15 years wages?

15 To one servant the Master gave the equal of 75 years' wages. To another 30 years' and to the third 15 years'. He gave to each according to his ability to use for the Master's profit, see 1 Thessalonians 2.4; 1 Corinthians 4.1,2; 1 Peter 4.10.

11-17 The first one got busy, put the money to work and doubled it. The second one did the same. They worked hard to please the Master, 1 John 3.22.

18,19 But the third servant was different. He did not love the Master, John 14.15. He really didn't know Him, v.24. So he disobeyed, dug a hole in the ground and buried the money instead of using it for the Master. The long time can refer to verse 5 again, and speaks of the present time of service, almost 2,000 years since the King went back to heaven. But suddenly the Master returned to settle accounts with the servants. This suggests the Judgment Seat of Christ, Romans 14.10-12; 1 Corinthians 3.10-15, when the believer's life and service will be reviewed and rewarded.

20-23 The first two servants pleased the Master and heard Him say, Well done! They were faithful, therefore they were rewarded. They would share the joy of their Master. What an encouragement this should be to believers today to faithfully serve Him. What has He entrusted to you? Write down a list of everything you can think of which He has given you. (Do you have anything you did not receive from Him? 1 Corinthians 4.7). Now write down by each item how much of it you have been using for Him. How does your list look now?

24,25 The third servant had put his money into **earthly** things (in the ground). He had done nothing for heavenly gain. He must have been ashamed to meet the Master, 1 John 2.28. He tries to cover up his laziness and neglect by blaming the Master for being a hard, cruel man. What an insult to the Master!

26,27 The Master called him a wicked and lazy servant. He asked him why he hadn't at least put the money in the bank to draw interest. The servant hadn't cared enough for the Master to do even that.

28-30 The wicked servant must be punished. He had insulted the Master, he had not loved and obeyed Him. He certainly had no faith in Him. Nor did he ask forgiveness for having neglected his duty. He himself was the hard man who had no respect or love. Love drives out fear, 1 John 4.18.

The Master took away what was entrusted to him and gave it to the other servant. Then he was driven out of the Master's house to regret his wasted life in sorrow and darkness, chapter 22.13. Important lesson for us: we will **lose** what we don't **use** for Christ. Rather may we use all we have and are for HIS glory.

The Sheep and Goats, 25.31-46

31-33 Now the King tells us about the future judgment of the Gentile nations who will be alive on earth when He comes in His glory to set up His Kingdom on earth. We must not confuse this with what we have just referred to in verse 19, the Judgment Seat of Christ which is for believers. Nor with the final Great White Throne judgment for the wicked dead, Revelation 20.11-15.

This judgment is at the Coming of the King when He will clean off from the earth all that is opposed to Him, see chapter 13.41. All the living nations will be called to account before the King of Kings. As He sets up His Kingdom He will remove all that is wrong and evil. He is going to rule in righteousness with a rod of iron, with justice and fairness, Psalm 2.9; Isaiah 32.1,17.

All people (Gentiles) will be divided into 2 groups. One is called sheep, the other goats. The sheep are the righteous, vs. 34,37. The goats are the wicked, v.41. The difference is not that some were "nice" people and the others "bad." But the test is what they did with the servants and message of the King.

Matthew 25.24-40   143

34-40 The righteous are invited to enter the inheritance of the Kingdom because they received, welcomed and cared for the King's messengers. These are called "my brothers" in verse 40. Chapter 12.50 tells us who they are: whoever does the will of the Father in heaven. The Church, believers of this present age, will have been taken to heaven at the Rapture, 1 Thessalonians 4.16-18. After that will come the period called the Great Tribulation, chapter 24. During that time the Lord will have other followers, converted Israelites, who will be preaching the Good News of the Kingdom, Revelation 6 and 7. What the nations will do with these messengers will really be what they do with the King who sent them.

To reject the messengers of the King is to reject the King Himself. Even the least important servant of the King should not be rejected. So the wicked will be punished and the righteous will share the blessings of the kingdom, chapter 13.42,43.

So the King has finished His "Olivet Discourse," outlining future events. Now He turns to the present—what is just ahead for Him—the Passover and Calvary.

Chapter 26

The King Betrayed and Condemned

In chapters 24 and 25 the King has been speaking about great sorrow and tribulation coming on the world. Now we read about the beginning of HIS sorrows as He nears Calvary. We see dark shadows of enemy hatred, but also bright shining of His true followers' love. The thoughts of many hearts are revealed, Luke 2.35:
>the bitter hatred of the rulers of Israel;
>the burning devotion of Mary;
>the bold bargaining of Judas;
>the blessed remembrance feast of love;
>the boastful words of Peter;
>the betrayal in the garden;
>the blind unbelief of the high priest; and
>the bitter weeping of a troubled Peter.

It all blends into a striking background behind the great beauty and perfection of the King Himself—His royal calm and dignity. He is not the victim of circumstances but Master of all. His enemies by wicked hands put Him to death but **only** because God had planned and allowed it all, Acts 2.23; John 10.17,18. Wonderful Savior yet King in control of all!

The Plot to Kill Jesus, 26.1-5

Who was plotting against Him? The chief priests and rulers, who should have been examples to the people. What were they plotting? Not merely to imprison Him or send Him out of the country, but to kill Him. Where were they plotting? In the high priest's palace. Caiaphas had been high priest since about A.D. 18. He should have been the spiritual leader of Israel, leading them to love and obey God. Instead he was fighting against God. When did they plot to kill Him? "Not during the Feast." But the King had said that it **would** be at Passover, v.2. And that **is** when He died. Wonderful King, in charge of His own death!

The Anointing at Bethany, 26.6-13

According to John 12 this took place six days before the Passover. So Matthew has taken this story out of order time-wise and put it here for a purpose. We believe it is because it lends great beauty to the background we mentioned earlier. It is a sharp contrast to the hatred and unbelief of the King's enemies.

1. *A Precious Sacrifice.* It was very costly for Mary. The perfume was nard from India and cost about a year's wages! She was only a woman of average means as far as we can tell, so this might have represented her life savings! But she brought it and broke the seal from the jar and poured it all out on her Lord Jesus. There was none left for herself. Beginning at His head and ending at His feet (John 12.3) she carefully emptied the jar on His dear body.

It was very precious to Christ also. He saw the motive in her heart was LOVE. She loved Him with all her heart. She understood when He said He was going to die and she believed His words (no one else did at that time). Mary's act of devotion is a picture of that of our Lord Himself. In His love to us He poured out His life as a sweet-smelling sacrifice to God on our behalf, Ephesians 5.2.

2. *A Pitiful Objection.* The disciples (led by Judas Iscariot) were angry at Mary. They called this act a "waste." They pretended to think about the poor people around them. How sadly their words condemned themselves. They thought more highly of money than they did of their Master. They wanted charity more than Christ. They called worship a waste.

Right here let us challenge our own hearts. Do we find it easy to agree with the disciples in this matter? Or do we take Mary's part and willingly give to our King a year's wages, or **all** we have?

3. *A Purposeful Act.* The King swiftly defended Mary. He calls her devotion BEAUTIFUL. To Him her faith was beautiful, she believed what He said about His death; her love was beautiful, it was totally unselfish; her action was beautiful, it was done with all her heart to prepare His body for burial—it was the proof of her faith and love.

4. *A Perpetual Memorial.* The fragrance of that perfume was no doubt still on His body as He went to the cross that week. And it surely lingered in Mary's own hair. But the real fragrance lasts until this day, recorded in the written Word of God. Worship always has a sweet and lasting fragrance. Any sacrifice for Christ is eternally remembered.

Only one life, it will soon be past—
Only what is done for Christ will **last.**

The Betrayer's Plot, 26.14-16

The betrayer was one of the twelve, very close to Jesus. This made his awful act even worse. See Psalm 55.12-14. He was called Judas Iscariot, which means, man of Kerioth, a town in Judea. He offered to hand Jesus over to the chief priests. But first he wanted to know how much they would give him. What a contrast this is to what we have just read about Mary:

Mary said, What can I do for **HIM**? (Love)

Judas said, What can I get for **me**? (Greed)

Of course the priests were happy, Mark 14.11. Here was just the opportunity they wanted, so they quickly agreed on the amount of money: 30 silver coins. If you look back at Exodus 21.32 you will find that was the price of a slave who had been killed by a bull! Those priests and Judas didn't realize how clearly their act pictured what really was taking place. Our Lord Jesus, the King of Glory, had willingly become a slave; look up Philippians 2.5-8 and read carefully. Then read the prophetic words of Psalm 22.11-18. Can you see the picture—the Slave violently wounded and killed by the fierce wild animals including the bull? Oh, what grace and love our blessed Savior showed to us!

The 30 silver coins are also referred to in Zechariah 11.12,13 but we will look at that when we come to chapter 27.

The Passover Feast, 26.17-25

It would be good for the reader to read Exodus 12 just now so as to better understand this section of our chapter. In Exodus 12.1-14 God gave directions to Moses for observing the first Passover. Then in verses 15-20 He gave directions for its future celebration. And in verses 21-27 Moses passed on the instructions to the people.

17-19 1. *Preparation.* We will give a brief outline of what scholars and historians have written about this great Passover Feast. According to Luke 22.8 John and Peter were the disciples who made the preparations. On the 14th day of Abib (later called Nisan—our April) the lamb was carried on their shoulders to the temple, to the court of priests, before the gate was closed at 1:30 PM. Three trumpets were blown to signal the time for killing the lamb. One man held the lamb while the other killed it. The priest caught the blood in a gold bowl. Another priest splashed the blood on the great altar of Burnt Offering, while Levites sang Psalms 113 and 114. The lamb was skinned and the inwards burned on the altar. Then the lamb was roasted on a pomegranate pole put through the whole length of the body. Then it was carried between Peter and John to the "guest room."

20-25 2. *Passover.* Four cups of wine were to be used. The head of the household or group would take the first cup, mix it with water, give thanks and pass it around to all, Luke 22.17. Dishes of bitter herbs were brought in and three loaves of unleavened bread. The herbs were dipped in vinegar or salt and eaten. The middle loaf of bread was broken, blessed and eaten. The second cup was mixed and filled. Then the youngest person present asked what this feast meant. The story of Exodus 1-12 would be re-told. The cup was lifted up, blessed and drunk. Psalms 115 and 116 were then sung. Next the roast lamb was brought in, served and eaten with a bowl full of bitter sauce. Morsels were dipped in and eaten. Then the third cup was mixed, filled, blessed and drunk as the feast closed, Luke 22.18.

21-25 While they were eating (the Passover) Jesus told the disciples about the betrayer. In great surprise they each asked, Is it I? Even Judas asked and Jesus answered that it was he. So Judas understood that Jesus knew him perfectly. He heard the King Himself say a most terrible thing about him: Better that he had never been born. This is true of all others who reject the Lord Jesus: It is better never to be born than never to be born again, John 3.3. Shortly after this Judas went out to get soldiers to capture Jesus.

The Lord's Supper, 26.26-30

As the Passover Feast was ending, the Lord Jesus took the remaining loaf and cup and used it in a new way. Symbolically the Passover was being fulfilled—this would be the last Passover. Christ our Passover was being sacrificed and would die on the cross in just a few hours, 1 Corinthians 5.7. No longer would God recognize that feast. It had pointed forward to the cross of Christ.

Now in view of His death as the True Passover Lamb (John 1.29) our Lord established a new Memorial Feast for His followers. Notice it is a time of thanksgiving—He gave thanks. So do His followers. Notice the symbolism:

1. **Bread** pictures His Body—given in voluntary sacrifice; broken—grain cut down, ground, baked in fire—speaking of God's judgment on our sin.

2. **Cup** — containing the fruit of the vine—pictures His precious Blood. The blood of the grape was pressed out in the winepress of judgment. It was poured out for the cleansing of our sins, Hebrews 9.22; 1 John 1.7.

Notice also the purpose of this feast:
(1) *A feast of commemoration:*
— a Memorial of a past, dying Friend
— a Remembrance of a present, living Friend
— a Reminder of a soon-coming Friend,
1 Corinthians 11.23-26

He called it a Remembrance of ME, Luke 22.19. We are asked to remember His Name, Psalm 20._____;
His marvelous works, 1 Chronicles 16. _____;
His love, Song of Solomon 1. _____;
His afflictions, Lamentations 3. _____;
His resurrection and exaltation, 2 Timothy 2. _____;
His words, Acts 20. _____.
Look up and fill in the verse references.

(2) *A Feast of Communion*, 1 Corinthians 10.16. It is a time of personal meeting with Christ; a time of close, warm fellowship and devotion to Him, our Lover and Savior.

(3) *A Feast of Covenant*—the new covenant, v.28. A time of renewed dedication and loyalty to Him, our King and Redeemer.

The Climax—they sang a hymn, probably the rest of the Hallel, Psalms 117 and 118. The closing words are, *Give thanks to the Lord for He is good, His love is forever*. With that music in their hearts they went out to the Mount of Olives and Gethsemane.

The Continuance—Ever since that night in that upper room Christ's true followers have gladly responded to His request, *Do this in remembrance of me*. To this very day many thousands of believers meet together each first day of the week to lovingly remember, worship and praise their wonderful and worthy Savior. Are you among them?

> On that same night, Lord Jesus, when all around you joined
> To cast its darkest shadows across your holy mind,
> We hear your voice, blest Savior, "Remember me—this do"
> With joyful hearts responding we do remember you!

A Sad Prediction, 26.31-35

Our Lord must have been very sorrowful when He told His disciples about the betrayer, in vs. 21-24. But He had another sorrow to share with them. **They** also were going to turn away from Him and leave Him. Again He quoted from the Old Testament, Zechariah 13.7. He Himself was the Shepherd who was going to be killed shortly. They were His sheep and would be scattered. This was fulfilled in verse 56. But He quickly promised that He was going to rise from the dead, and He said He would go ahead of them into Galilee.

However, Peter and the other 10 replied that they would never turn away or leave Him. They loved Him too much for that! (or so they thought). But the Lord told Peter that on that very night he would say three times that he didn't know Jesus. Peter had to learn never to boast about himself. But at this time he didn't believe his Master's words. He boldly said the very opposite, Even if I have to die with You, I will never leave or deny You! All the other disciples said the same thing. Noble words and easy to say, but impossible to fulfill in one's own strength.

Gethsemane, 26.36-46

Jesus and His disciples went out of the city and crossed the Kidron valley. They went up the slopes of the Mount of Olives to an enclosed olive orchard called Gethsemane. Jesus had often gone there to pray in the quiet, cool shade of the olive trees, John 18.1,2. Evidently there was an olive press in that place since the name Gethsemane means, Place of the Olive Press, or Enclosed place. That was where the olive oil was squeezed out of the olives in proper season. But this night there was going to be another kind of crushing. Awful pressure was coming on the heart and spirit of our dear Lord.

This time in Gethsemane was like the Temple which had three main sections: the outer court, the Holy Place, and the Most Holy Place. In verse 36 our Lord left eight of His disciples near the entrance of the olive orchard (like the outer court). In verse 37 He took three of them, Peter, James, and John, farther in (like the Holy Place) to explain to them the awful sorrow that was coming on His holy soul. But in verse 39 He left them and went on farther to be all alone with God His Father as in the most holy place.

In the Holy Place of the temple the priests offered incense (prayer) to God. Here in Gethsemane the three disciples were told to watch and pray, vs. 38 and 41. In verses 37 and 38 three words describe a terrible, heavy sorrow which was coming on Him. The first word is translated: sorrowful, hurt, terribly sad, in anguish. The next word: very heavy, greatly distressed, deeply troubled. In verse 38 an even stronger word: surrounded by sorrow, swallowed up by distress, deeply grieved, even to the point of death. Luke 22.44 adds that His sweat became like drops of blood falling to the ground. All of this tells us just a little bit of how deeply Christ was suffering as He prayed in agony to His Father in the Most Holy Place.

Reverently we ask, WHY was this such intense sorrow? What was the great weight which crushed His holy soul? Listen to His prayer—three times He mentions, "This cup." What does this refer to? In John 18.11 He later asked, "Shall I not drink the cup My Father has given Me?" Now in our chapter He asks the Father to remove that cup from Him. Many times in the Old Testament the "cup" refers to judgment. Here are a few examples to look up: Psalm 75.8; Isaiah 51.17; Jeremiah 25.15,28; Ezekiel 23.31-33; also see Revelation 14.10. These would suggest that "this cup" refers to God's holy, angry judgment upon sin. It was **our** sin which was laid on HIM.

That judgment is too awful for us to describe. But it was even more awful for our blessed Savior. There were at least three main elements mixed into that cup which caused Him such intense suffering:

1. *His great horror of sin.* Remember He was the spotless, holy One, Hebrews 9.14; 1 Peter 1.19. He knew no sin, 2 Corinthians 5.21. In Him was no sin, 1 John 3.5. He did no sin, 1 Peter 2.22. Yet He was about to be "made sin" for us. His holy soul shrank from that. Think of how good you feel when you are bathed and clean and have your best new clothes on. Then think of someone throwing you into the sewage ditch to drown there. That is only a very, very faint picture of the awful horror Jesus felt against sin.

2. *He was to experience the curse of our sin,* Galatians 3.13. Sweat was one result of the curse, Genesis 3.19. He, the blessed One, was to be made a curse (be cursed) for us. As He peered through the dark night toward His holy Father He knew He was going to be abandoned. That was the sharpest thorn of the curse—no answer from God, chapter 27.46.

3. *He was being attacked by Satan and all his demons.* In Luke 22.53 He saw that Satan and the powers of darkness were coming against Him. Also see John 14.30. We can never understand how they attacked and tormented His holy soul that night.

Now all this suffering was in Gethsemane. He was not at Calvary yet. Gethsemane was only like the steps leading up to the altar of sacrifice (the cross). On the cross He suffered for our sins, that is Redemption. Here in Gethsemane it is only in anticipation, that is, a foretaste of what was to come. Here His prayer is that of Submission. Since there is no other way by which mankind could be saved from sin, He will go to Calvary. He has sweat blood but there He must **shed** His blood, Hebrews 9.22. So He prays, "Father, let Your will be done."

Three times He repeated those blessed words, and three times He went back to find His disciples sleeping. He asked Peter about that but he had no reply, no doubt because of shame as he remembered what he had said in verse 35. Then, hearing the crowd coming, Jesus said to them, "Here comes My betrayer. Get up and let's go!" Where did He go? Did He run away from the enemy? NO! He went TO them, John 18.4. (Compare David running in 1 Samuel 17.48.)

The King Arrested, 26.47-56

47 The Betrayer. Judas is called here — one of the twelve. He had been that, but now he is one of a large crowd. It was made up of: (1) Roman soldiers with their commander, John 18.12, armed with swords; (2) Jewish temple guards, police armed with clubs; (3) some chief priests and elders of Israel, Luke 22.52.

48 The Signal. A kiss! They were to arrest the one Judas kissed.

49 The Act. Judas went straight to Jesus, greeted Him and kissed Him as if he really loved Him. Some Bible teachers have pointed out that it was very improper for a disciple to greet his master first because it suggested they were equals. In fact it really was an insult and amounted to a denial of their previous relationship.

50 The Arrest. The Master showed only grace toward His wayward follower. He called him "Friend." But was not Judas His enemy? Yes, but Jesus was not Judas's enemy. The hatred was all on the part of Judas. The love was all on our Lord's part, chapter 5.44. Then the soldiers grabbed Jesus and arrested Him.

51-54 The Defense. At once Peter (John 18.10) pulled his sword and started swinging at them. One of the high priest's servants ducked his head just in time—his ear was cut off instead of his head! His name was Malchus, John 18.10. But Jesus didn't need Peter's protection nor any other man's. He is the KING. He had authority to call for more than 12 armies of angels. The enemy crowd would have been helpless. But He reminded them that the Scripture must be fulfilled. (Another "identity picture": see note on v. 56.)

> He **could** have called 70 thousand angels
> To destroy them all and set Him free;
> He could have called all those angels
> But He **didn't** —He died alone to set **me** free!

Hallelujah, what a Savior!

55,56 The Rebuke. Jesus then talked to the crowd: Why did you bring so many men and weapons? Did you come to capture a wild, violent criminal? They could have found Him any day peacefully teaching the people in the temple. But the Scriptures must be fulfilled. For example, look up Psalm 22. Write down which verses you think would fit in here. Do the same with Psalm 41 and 55.

When the disciples saw what was happening they **all** deserted Him and ran away. (What about verse 31—do you think they remembered?)

The Jewish Trial, 26.57-68

In John 18.12-23 we read that they first took Jesus to Annas, the ex-high priest. He was old and his son-in-law, Caiaphas, was high priest that year. Annas held only a preliminary hearing and sent Jesus to Caiaphas. (The two priests probably lived in the same house with a courtyard between.) The whole Sanhedrin (*see footnote) was already there, by a previous plan, no doubt. It was midnight or later but that didn't hinder them from their evil plans. At last they have Jesus as a prisoner. They are determined to get rid of Him—put Him to death, v.59.

But they had to do it "legally." A guilty verdict must be based on evidence, but there was no evidence. So they started looking for false witnesses. (If they can't have truth on their side they will use lies.) They had trouble finding two liars to agree on one statement, v.60; Deuteronomy 17.6. At last, v.61, two agreed that He had said that He was able to destroy the temple of God and rebuild it in three days. But see John 2.19,21 and note how they twisted what He said.

62,63 Jesus was silent to these false charges. He knew they would not accept what He said because their minds were already made up, John 2.24,25. Then the high priest put Jesus under solemn oath (see Leviticus 5.1) saying, by the living God, "Tell us if you are Messiah, the Son of God." (See Psalm 2.2,7 for "identity picture" here.)

64 Now comes the most important statement Jesus ever made concerning Himself—it can be called His Great Confession. He is the Faithful and True Witness (Revelation 3.14). He answered, "Yes, it is true, I am the Messiah, the Christ, the Son of God." How thankful we are to hear His clear statement—He **is** the Son of God. Let all present-day doubters stop doubting who Jesus is. Fall at His feet and worship HIM!

Then Jesus added another "identity picture" —from Daniel 7.13,14 and Psalm 110.1,2. The lowly, despised prisoner standing before the Sanhedrin was going to come back in glory and reign over this earth—the Son of Man and Son of God. Wise people believe and bow the knee to Him now, Psalm 2.10-12.

65 But that was not what Caiaphas and the 70 did that night. The high priest tore his clothes and screamed, "He has blasphemed!" Tearing one's clothes was a common sign of great grief or distress. But the high priest was forbidden to do that, Leviticus 21.10. So Caiaphas broke God's law in front of the whole council. He should have been replaced at once, but he wasn't. Instead he appealed to the council, "What is your decision?" They answered that Jesus was worthy of the death sentence.

*Footnote: The Sanhedrin was the supreme ruling council and high court of Israel. It was made up of 70 members plus the high priest who was president. Members were chief priests, elders and doctors of the law. See Numbers 11.16,24,25.

67 Now we can hardly believe what we read next: **They,** the priests and religious leaders of Israel came up to the Son of God and spit in His face, struck Him with their fists, and mocked and slapped Him. How could they? Such is the sinful human heart, even the "religious" heart. Luke 22.64 tells us that they blindfolded Him first. Perhaps they couldn't stand the look of pity and love in His eyes. What love and grace He showed, with never a murmur or complaint.

And why did He allow all this? We believe He caused them to ask the question, "Who hit you?" They were having a game with Him. But the whole world must hear this important question: Who really was smiting Christ? Behind the mocking cruelty of those Jews, behind the poisonous hatred of Satan and his demons—there is another Hand at work here. Jesus Christ is not being punished and tormented for His own sins. He is not suffering as a Martyr for a good cause. Let the prophet Isaiah tell the real truth: "He was wounded for our sins, He was bruised because of evil we did. **The Lord** laid on Him the punishment all of us deserved," Isaiah 53.5,6.

Peter Denies Jesus, 26.69-75

Peter loved his Lord greatly. He was willing to die for Him. He took his own life in his hand to defend Jesus, v. 51. True, he forsook Him (they all did), v.56. But his love made him go back to follow (at a distance) and then go right into the courtyard to watch the trial. There was true love in Peter's heart to make him do that.

But the mistake he made was in boasting, v.35. His self-confidence would have to be replaced by confidence in Christ, Philippians 3.3. All Christians need to learn this lesson sooner or later, and the sooner the better. This is one reason Peter's experience here is included in the chapter. You and I need to learn from Peter.

First a servant girl, then another servant girl, then some of the soldiers—three times they accused Peter of being a follower of Jesus. Three times he denied, the last time calling down curses on himself. Then that rooster crowed, just as Jesus had predicted. Peter remembered. Only those who have experienced this kind of thing can understand how badly Peter felt. He left the courtyard at once and went somewhere to weep bitterly: tears of repentance, tears of love, tears of victory in defeat. He had learned his lesson.

One Bible teacher wrote: Love at a distance and curious—that was Peter's failure; love challenged and cowardly—that was the devil's sifting; love remembering and contrite—that was Christ's victory.

Chapter 27

The King Crucified

It was early in the morning when the Council decided to put Jesus to death. So they tied His hands and led Him off to Pilate the Roman Governor. And so ended the Jewish "religious" trial of the King. We must pause here to note some important things which were wrong about this mock trial:

1. The judges had made up their mind to condemn the prisoner before the trial even started, chapter 26.4,59.

2. They **looked** for false evidence (because there was no truth in them), v.59.

3. They knowingly accepted two liars as "witnesses," v.60.

4. The two liars twisted the words of Jesus, v.61; John 2.19,21.

5. According to their own Jewish law the Council was not allowed to try capital crimes at night.

6. Also it was against their law to pass capital sentence (death) on the same day as the trial.

7. It was also illegal to execute a prisoner on the same day the sentencing was made.

8. The high priest was forbidden to tear his clothing, Leviticus 21.10.

9. They were not allowed to try any prisoner on the Sabbaths or the Feast days.

10. They abused and tortured their defenseless prisoner, v.67.

The End of Judas the Traitor, 27.3-10

Perhaps Judas had expected that Jesus would miraculously free Himself from the Jews. Instead he saw that they condemned Him to die and He did not try to free Himself nor to set up His kingdom at once. Then Judas became sorry that he had betrayed Jesus. He was filled with remorse but it did not lead him to repentance. It only brought death, see 2 Corinthians 7.9,10. If he had only turned to Jesus and confessed his sin he would have been forgiven, see Luke 23.34,43. But Judas did not have faith in the Savior. Contrast Peter's godly sorrow of faith, chapter 26.75.

4 Instead Judas went to the chief priests and confessed, "I have sinned and have betrayed innocent blood." He said the truth but he said it to the wrong persons, the priests. They were supposed to show God's love and kindness to the people. But they with hard hearts simply told him that that was **his** problem! That is just how Satan treats his followers—he dumps them when he has finished using them!

5 The money was "burning" in Judas's hand; his crime was "burning" in his conscience. He must get rid of it all (he had not used one coin of the money). He tried to return it to the priests but they wouldn't take it. So as they went back into the temple he threw the 30 coins after them. However that didn't ease his conscience. In deep misery and remorse all he could think of was to end it all, so he went out and hanged himself. (But that didn't end the "burning." Read Matthew 25.41; Acts 1.25 and Revelation 19.20.)

6 The priests couldn't leave the coins strewn around the temple floor. They had to keep a "clean house" so they picked up the coins. But neither could they put the money in the temple treasury because it was "unclean" money and the Old Testament forbad putting unclean money into the temple. Their hands were stained with blood and now this blood-money was "burning" in their hands and they must get rid of it.

7,8 Near the potter's gate of the city, by the valley of Hinnon, there was a potter's field for sale. The many holes where the clay had been dug out could be used for graves. They decided this would make a good burying ground for the Gentile strangers among them who could not be buried in Jewish cemeteries. So they used this "blood money" to buy that potter's field. It became known as the Field of Blood.

9,10 Again Matthew makes reference to Old Testament scripture. More than Jeremiah is quoted here. The whole chapter is referred to regarding Jeremiah, and then these direct words are quoted from the prophet Zechariah. Notice the references:

v. 3 refers to chief priests and elders Compare Jer. 19.1
      to innocent blood Compare Jer. 19.4
vs. 5-7 — money for buying (a pot) Compare Jer. 19.1
    —to a potter Compare Jer. 19.1 and 18.1-4
Potter's gate was at valley of Hinnon Compare Jer. 19.2
references to a field Compare Jer. 32.6-15
    bought with silver Compare Jer. 32.25.

But then Matthew quotes directly from another prophet, Zechariah 11.12 where we read about the exact amount of the silver, 30 pieces. And in 11.13 he mentions throwing them to the potter in the Lord's house (temple). And Matthew 27.10 sums it up by showing that all of this took place "as the Lord planned" (it was not just by chance).

The Roman Trial, 27.11-26

Pontius Pilate was the Roman Governor over Judea from A.D. 26-36. The Jewish Council turned Jesus over to Pilate for execution. Some teachers say that this is because the Jews were not permitted to put anyone to death. But see Acts 7.54-60. Others feel that the Jews wanted to pass on the responsibility to Rome. In any case the Bible clearly tells us that both Jews and Gentiles are responsible and that it was all according to God's plan and purpose, Acts 2.22,23.

The Jewish trial had been on religious issues: blasphemy, messiahship and deity of Jesus.

The Roman trial takes up the political issue. Luke and John tell us how the priests charged that Jesus was a revolutionary, a rival to Caesar, an evil doer. There are seven charges the Jews made against Christ. Look up these references and write down each charge:

Matthew 26.61 _____
Luke 23.2 _____
Luke 23.2 _____
Luke 23.2 _____
Luke 23.5 _____
John 18.30 _____
John 19.7 _____

The Jews knew it was Pilate's job to uphold Caesar and put down any rival king. Matthew is presenting Jesus as King all through this book, so he records Pilate's first question to Jesus: Are you the King of the Jews? Jesus clearly answered, Yes, it is as you say.

12-14 But when the chief priests and rulers made many accusations against Jesus, He never answered one of them (they were false charges). This surprised Pilate greatly. Again we note the King was silent when falsely accused in chapter 26.63, and we read here twice that He did not answer. When we ask, WHY? we realize He was taking our place. He had no sin but He was charged with our sin, 2 Corinthians 5.21.

Why was He silent when a word would slay His accusers all?
Why does He meekly bear their taunts when angels await His call?
"He was made sin"—my sin He bore upon the accursed tree;
And **sin has no defense to make**—His silence was for **me!**

(Selected)

15-18 *A Choice to Make.* Pilate remembered his custom of releasing to the people a prisoner each year at the Feast time. Barabbas (meaning "son of the father") was a well-known criminal who was in prison for robbery and revolt against the government (probably along with two other criminals like him, Mark 15.7). They were sitting on "death row" awaiting execution. Pilate knew the Jews had no love for Jesus but he thought they would love Barabbas even less. So he told them to choose which one they wanted to be set free, criminal Barabbas or Christ Jesus.

19 *A Dream.* Then evidently Pilate went inside to talk more with Jesus (as in John 18.33-38). Just then an urgent message came to Pilate from his wife. She had had a frightening dream about Jesus and she urged Pilate to leave that good, innocent Prisoner alone. Who caused her to have that dream? We are sure God did, Job 33.14-17. (Do you remember three dreams in Matthew 2?) Would Pilate take the advice of his wife?

By this time Pilate was realizing more and more that he had a real problem. He knew Jesus was innocent and that the Jews hated Jesus and were demanding His death. He hoped they would choose Barabbas.

20-25 *The Mob.* Meanwhile the priests had stirred up all the people against Jesus. So when Pilate went out and asked them whom they had chosen they shouted, Barabbas. Then he asked a very important question—for him and for all of us: What shall I do with Jesus? What is **your** answer to that question?

> *Jesus is standing on trial yet*
> *Will you try to evade Him like Pilate?*
> *Or will you choose to receive Him by faith?*
> *What will you do with Jesus?*
> *Neutral you cannot be—*
> *Someday your heart will be asking*
> *What will HE do with me?*

The mob's answer to Pilate's question was one loud roar: Crucify Him—nail Him to a cross. Pilate challenged them—what crime had He committed? Only a louder roar, Put Him on a cross! By now Pilate saw a riot was beginning. He must act at once. His conscience told him that Jesus was innocent. (Note seven times Jesus was declared "not guilty" by His judges as recorded in the four Gospels. Find and mark these references.) Pilate was afraid—but it was fear of man (Caesar) and fear of losing his job and reputation, not fear of God. But there was no time to waste. So hurriedly he called for a basin of water and washed his hands in front of the mob, saying, I am innocent of this man's blood—it's now your responsibility.

What a mistake he made! He thought water could wash away the guilt of murder. Never! Only Christ's blood can cleanse from sin. (Read an interesting story which illustrates all of this in Deuteronomy 21.1-9.) Pilate's wife said Jesus was innocent, v. 19. Pilate himself admitted it, too, Luke 23.4,15. But he could **not** call himself innocent, v.26.

25 The mob answered, Let His blood be on us and on our children.

So the Jews admitted their share of guilt. Little did they realize that in only a few years (A.D.70) God would begin to take them at their word. Many thousands of Jews were horribly killed by the Romans at the fall of Jerusalem.

Oh, what a sad, bad choice both Jews and Gentiles made! The world chose to have Barabbas and rejected Jesus. They chose a murderer, robber, revolutionary, and the world has had murders, robberies and wars ever since. They rejected the Prince of Peace and have never had peace since.

26 *The Official Sentence:* Barabbas freed and Jesus condemned. So there was a great exchange made that day. A guilty sinner was set free and an Innocent Savior was put to death in place of the guilty one (and all of us guilty ones). What love He showed!

But before Pilate handed Jesus over to die He ordered that He be whipped. We must not pass over this quickly—it was a terrible suffering Jesus endured. We would only quote a brief description by an old writer (Krummacher): "Look at yonder pillar, black with blood of murderers and rebels. The iron collar which is attached to it, as well as the ropes which hang down from its iron rings. . . . Look at the rude and barbarous beings . . . who busily surround their victim. Observe the instruments of torture in their hands. They are scourges, made of hundreds of leather thongs each armed at the point with a bony hook or sharp-sided cube . . . The executioners fall on the Holy One like a host of devils. They tear off His clothes, bind those hands which were ever stretched out to do good, tie them together behind His back, press His gracious face firmly against the shameful pillar. After having tied Him with ropes in such a manner that He cannot move or stir, they begin their cruel task . . . I could not count to you the number of strokes now poured on His sacred body, nor describe the torments increasing with every stroke. In some cases they caused the death of the unhappy victim! It is enough for us to know it lasted fully a quarter of an hour. Streams of blood flow from His sacred form, yet the scourging continues without mercy. There is not a nerve of the divine Sufferer that does not hurt with nameless pain and smart. But such is the intention. The scourges cut ever deeper into the wounds already made and penetrate almost to the bones. His whole back appears an enormous wound."

It is not a wonder that this whipping-scourging was called the Halfway Death. All this fulfilled other Old Testament prophecies—see Psalm 129.3, Isaiah 50.6. Oh how He suffered! Oh how He loved you and me! Thank and praise Him right now.

Mocking the King, 27.27-31

The Praetorium was where the governor lived and was the headquarters of the soldiers. The whole cohort, or company, of 600 soldiers now gathered around their new Prisoner. They were ordered to take Jesus and nail Him to a cross. But before doing so they wanted to have some cruel "fun" with Him. They played a game "Hail to the King." They took an old used officer's robe of red or purple. After taking off Jesus' clothes they put this on Him. Some made a crown of long, sharp thorns (Genesis 3.17-19) which grew nearby. They put it on His head and a reed in His hand. Then they knelt before Him mocking, Hail King of the Jews. They spit in His face and kept hitting Him over the head driving the thorns deeply into His forehead and face. What a sight it was! Was He really a King? Blood was flowing from His back and head, sweat and spittle were on His swollen, bruised face. Can this be a King? Who would recognize Him as the Creator and Ruler of the Universe? (Isaiah 52.13-15). Can this be HE? Yes, this is He, — and this is love, love unimagined and unknown!

When the soldiers got tired of their cruel mockery they put Jesus' clothing back on Him and led Him away to the place of execution outside the city. He went willingly.

The King on a Cross, 27.32-44

32 Our blessed Lord must have been very tired and weak after all those sufferings. On the way out of the city the soldiers must have seen Him falter and stagger. Perhaps He even fell down under the heavy load of the cross. The Bible doesn't say. But the soldiers stopped a man from Africa, Simon by name. They forced him to carry the cross for Jesus. We are not told whether or not Simon became a Christian later. See Mark 15.21.

33 Finally they arrived at the Place of the Skull ("Golgotha" in the Aramaic language; "Calvary" in Latin). This was probably a mound or rocky place which looked like a skull. The only other references in the Bible to a skull both speak of violence: Judges 9.53; 2 Kings 9.35.

34 Jesus was offered a drink of wine-vinegar mixed with gall, which was a drug to deaden pain. But Jesus refused it. He wanted to suffer all the pain fully awake. He did not want to dull His feelings nor His communion with His Father. He had another cup to drink, spiritually—the cup of God's anger against our sins. (Refer to notes on chapter 26.36-46.)

35 With the cross lying on the ground they took off Jesus' clothes and laid Him on it, and spiked His hands and feet to it. Then raising it up they dropped it into the hole in the ground. There He hung, **lifted up** between heaven and earth. Four times in John we read about His being lifted up. Find these verses in John chapters 3,8 and 12. The soldiers were allowed to divide up the prisoner's belongings, so they gambled for His clothing (that's all He had!) Again Old Testament prophecies were fulfilled, Psalm 22.16,18.

36-38 Then they sat down to keep guard over Him (so none of His friends could come and take Him down from the cross). They had also nailed two robbers on crosses—one on each side of Jesus. Over each cross was a sign stating the crime that person had committed. What was Jesus' crime? "This is Jesus the King of the Jews." How amazing! At His birth it was announced He was a King, Matthew 2.2. And here at His death He is called the King! And that has been Matthew's theme all through his book: The KING, Jesus.

39,40 The Place of the Skull was on a busy road going into the city.
    Many people passed by, some shouting insults at Him, Come down from the cross if you are the Son of God. They shook their heads. See Psalm 22.7.

41,42 The chief priests and rulers also came by and mocked Him.
    They jeered and sneered at Him, saying, He saved others but can't save Himself. But they were actually speaking a beautiful truth. He really could not save Himself **and** others.

Himself He could not save, He on the cross must die,
Or mercy could not come to ruined sinners nigh.
Yes, Christ the Son of God must bleed
That sinners might from sin be freed.

43 Wickedly they even quoted from the Old Testament about God delighting in Him or not, Psalm 18.16-19; 41.11; 22.8.

44 The two robbers joined in heaping insults on Him, although later one of them repented and was saved, Luke 23.39-43. The soldiers also came up and mocked Him, Luke 23.36,37. And through it all did you notice the Silence of the King? Never a reply or murmur. Look at Peter's comment on this in 1 Peter 2.21-25. Do you see a lesson for us?

But do you marvel more at the silence of God during all this? Do you wonder why those 70 thousand angels held back and did not strike down all those wicked sinners? God held the angels back, because there was no other way by which lost sinners could be saved. God **SO** loved the world of mankind that He **gave** His beloved Son so that whoever believes in Him would not perish but have eternal life (John 3.16). Do you believe that?

Could Jesus have come down from the cross? NO, because His **love** held Him there. "The Son of God **loved** me and **gave** Himself for me," Galatians 2.20.

> *To Calvary's hill, one day, the Lord was led away*
> *None else the price could pay for all my sin.*
> *It was His love for me that nailed Him to the tree*
> *To die in agony for all my sin.*
> *Was ever love so strong? Was ever crime so wrong?*
> *When Jesus suffered long for all my sin.*
> *Oh, what a Savior is mine!*
> *In Him God's mercies combine,*
> *His love can never decline—and HE loves **me**!*
>
> (Clayton)

The Death of the King, 27.45-56

45 God was silent during all this, but He was not idle or inactive.

The first sign-miracle He sent was a heavy darkness to cover the horror of that scene. At mid-day it became midnight, Amos 8.9,10. Mankind had been watching and mocking for three hours. Now they would be allowed to see no more until about 3 PM. During those awful three hours God poured on His Son His terrible anger against our sins. See Isaiah 53.5; 2 Corinthians 5.21.

46 Jesus spoke seven times while He was on the cross. Look up and write down what He said: Luke 23.34,43; John 19.26; Matthew 27.46; John 19.28,30; Luke 23.46. Matthew records only the central, fourth saying. Our Savior quoted the first verse of Psalm 22. Here is another "identity picture" of prophecy. The bodily sufferings of the first three hours become like nothing compared to the spiritual sufferings of these last three hours. We cannot understand how painful it was for Him to bear our sins. But He utters the deepest pain of His heart in that word, "forsaken." It is the only means we have of measuring the true depths of Calvary-love. God loves His Son with a measureless love, Matthew 3.17; 17.5. The Son loves His Father equally. But God loved us sinners SO much that He punished Him instead of us. He had to forsake Him, that is leave Him alone. And it was His love to us which caused it!

Measured by that cross, that darkness,
O how deep God's love must be;
Deep as were Christ's depths of anguish,
Is the Father's love for me!

47-49 The word "My God" in Aramaic sounded like the name Elijah. Someone thought Jesus was calling for Elijah. You may remember that Elijah had not died but was taken alive up to heaven, 2 Kings 2. He had appeared with Moses on the Mount of Transfiguration, chapter 17.3. Perhaps they thought that with power from God Elijah might deliver Jesus. Compare 1 Kings 18 and 2 Kings 1.9-15.

Meanwhile John 19.28 records that Jesus had cried out, I am thirsty! So someone put some of the soldiers' wine-vinegar (not the drugged vinegar of verse 34) on a sponge and held it up to Jesus on a reed. This fulfilled Psalm 69.21. Others told him to leave Jesus alone, they wanted to see if Elijah would really come.

50 Jesus cried out with a loud voice. John 19.30 tells us what He said: IT IS FINISHED. It was the victory shout of the King. Redemption's work is forever completed. Hallelujah!

Then Jesus dismissed His spirit and died. He literally laid down His life, as He promised in John 10.17,18. His work was done, He had glorified His Father, John 17.4,5,13.

And so there He died, the KING CRUCIFIED
To save a poor sinner like me.

51 Immediately God acted. At the moment of the King's death God worked a double sign. First He tore in two the great curtain which hung between the Holy Place and the Most Holy Place in the temple. See Exodus 26.31-35. Only the high priest was allowed to pass into the Most Holy Place once a year on the Day of Atonement.

The Great Curtain said, as it were, to all, Keep Out! You cannot come near to God because of your sin, Hebrews 9.8. But Hebrews 10.19-23 explains the meaning of what happened when Jesus died. God tore the curtain away and says to believers, Now you may come near to Me through the blood of Jesus. The torn curtain also meant the end of Judaism-religion of the Old Testament. Christ was beginning a New work, a New Covenant. See Hebrews 8.

52,53 The second sign God gave was a great earthquake which shook the earth, broke rocks into pieces and broke open the graves of many godly people. These probably were believers in Jesus who had died before His death. See 1 Thessalonians 4.14. When Jesus arose from the dead they also arose from their graves and went into the holy city (Jerusalem) and appeared to many people there. Perhaps this was a partial fulfillment of Isaiah 26.19 and Ezekiel 37.12,13.

Matthew is the only one who records this event and he writes very little about it. So there are difficult questions unanswered. Did they go into heaven when Jesus ascended? Could Hebrews 2.13 and Isaiah 8.17,18 refer to them? We are not sure.

54 But the earthquake shook more than earth and rocks. The Roman officer and his soldiers were shaken also. They were terrified. Never had they seen such a death before. They admitted that Jesus must have been God's Son. And they were right!

55,56 Here we read about some other watchers. Faithful women were watching from a distance. All the disciples had fled. Probably most of the crowds of people had also hurried home when the awful darkness came (Luke 23.48). But these brave women had stayed through it all. They loved Jesus deeply. They had followed Him all the way from Galilee in order to help care for Him. Only three are named. Would you have been standing with them if you lived then?

Royal Burial, 27.57-61

John 19 tells us that the Jewish rulers did not want bodies left hanging on crosses overnight. See Deuteronomy 21.22,23. And the next day was a special Sabbath. So they asked Pilate to have all three prisoners put to death before evening. Then the soldiers would take the bodies down and throw them into a common, criminal's grave. But God was not going to allow that. The King was to have an honorable burial.

57,58 JOSEPH, a member of the Council, was an honorable man who had not voted to put Jesus to death, Luke 23.50. He was a secret disciple of Jesus and had been afraid to speak out for Him, John 19.38. But now his faith shines very brightly in the surrounding darkness. The other disciples had fled and gone home in despair. Their hopes were totally broken—their King was dead. In this darkest hour Joseph hurried to Pilate's palace and asked permission to have the body of Jesus. Pilate must have been surprised at such a request from an honorable man like Joseph. But he granted Joseph's request (after he had made sure that Jesus was really dead, Mark 15.44,45).

59,60 Nicodemus joined Joseph, John 19.39. Carefully and lovingly they took the precious body off the cross. They wrapped it in clean linen cloth with some spices Nicodemus had brought (John 19). But it was almost dark. They would have to finish the embalming later, after the Sabbath was past (see Luke 24.1). Joseph was rich and his own new tomb was nearby in a garden (John 19). So they laid the body temporarily there. A stone was rolled in front of the entrance and they went home.

61 Again we find two women watching. And God was watching, too. He was fulfilling the Old Testament prophecy of Isaiah 53.9. They (men) had appointed Jesus' body to be buried with the wicked criminals, but God arranged that He was to be among the rich in His death. God was arranging for an honorable burial by honorable men for His Most Honorable Son, the King!

The Royal Honor Guard, 27.62-66

But God had still more honor to bestow on that grave. He caused the enemies of Jesus to arrange for a military guard to stand watch over the precious body. Of course, **they** didn't plan it for that reason. The chief priests and rulers asked Pilate for a guard to keep the body of Jesus from being stolen by the disciples. They remembered He had said something about rising from the dead on the third day. (It's interesting that the King's enemies had listened to that promise while His followers had forgotten or ignored it.)

Pilate didn't want Jesus to rise from the dead any more than did the chief priests. So Pilate's answer is a classic summary of the situation: Make the tomb as sure as you possibly can! And they did! When they had made sure the body was still in the grave they used all the security they could get: the Roman seal on the entrance and the Roman soldiers on guard day and night. These represented the greatest power on earth at that time. It was a majestic sight. Anyone passing by that beautiful garden must have wondered what important person was buried there. It was the King of Kings and Lord of Lords.

The Roman soldiers were the Royal Honor Guard until they were replaced by the Angels.

Chapter 28
The Risen King

The Risen King

Thank God, chapter 27 is not the end of Matthew's book. Nor of the King. He died but He didn't stay dead. He couldn't.

1 After the Sabbaths, or In the end of the Sabbaths. You will notice the plural form which is the literal translation. That week was a special sabbath-week: the sabbath of the Passover, Exodus 12.16; then the sabbath of Unleavened bread, followed by the week-sabbath, 7th day. That is why Matthew wrote, After the sabbaths had passed. But there is more. The whole system of Old Testament law-keeping was past. A New Order was being introduced, the First Day of the Week was dawning. Contrast the old and the new:

The old, Sabbath (Saturday)	The new, First day of week (Sunday)
End of the old week	Beginning of the new week
Spoke of finished creation (Genesis 2.23)	Finished Redemption, John 19.30
Day of Legal Obligation	Day of voluntary worship / service
Death for disobedience (Numbers 15.32-36)	Resurrection, Life abundant
Faded and passed into the night	Dawn of New Day — Light

So the first day of the week, the Lord's Day, for the Church, took the place of the 7th day sabbath. In a real sense the sunset was at Calvary when the Light of the world was rejected, put out. Then followed midnight darkness, death, defeat and despair (Luke 24.21). But the Resurrection of the King was the turning point toward the Dawning of New Day:

Darkness turned into Light, v.3
Death turned into Life, v.6
Defeat turned into Victory, (Satan destroyed, Hebrews 2.14; Death defeated, 2 Timothy 1.10)
Despair turned into Hope - John 14.19
        Joy - v.8; Great Joy, Luke 24.41,52
        Promise - v.7. You shall see Him.

- - - - - - - - - -

1 Again we see the faithful women watchers. They watched at His death, 27.55; at His burial, 27.61; now His resurrection, vs. 1-7.

What drew them to the tomb at this early hour? Mark and Luke tell us they were going to finish embalming the body of their beloved Lord. It was their LOVE to Him that drew them. The stone, the soldiers, the seal, none of these could scare them away. Love is strong as death, burning like a raging fire; many waters can't put it out, Song of Solomon 8.6,7. They were hopeless, disappointed, heart-broken and sad, but they came in Love. And Christ values our love above all else. See John 21.15; 1 Corinthians 16.22. And He reveals Himself to love, v.9.

2   Suddenly there was a violent earthquake. One of God's mighty angels came down from heaven, rolled the stone away and **sat** on it. Not only was the earth shaken, so also was the grave, death and hell. The death and resurrection of the King combine as the greatest events in history. Death and hell have been defeated and robbed of their power. Satan himself has been totally overcome, Hebrews 2.14,15; 2 Timothy 1.10. Look at that angel sitting on that stone, the symbol of the Power of Heaven. What scorn and contempt for those puny soldiers, for the seal of Rome, for the very power of death! It reminds us of Psalm 2.4,5, heaven laughing at its enemies.

The stone was large, 27.60, but it was rolled away. That stone was like:

1. a **millstone** of sin around our necks, sinking us into eternal judgment. But it has been removed—our sins are forgiven—gone!

2. a **tombstone** —the grave is where death reigned, but now death has been conquered. The tombstone has been removed, death and the grave have no final power over the believer, "Because I live—you shall!"

3. a **stumblingstone** —of doubt, fear and hopelessness. This too has been rolled away. Faith rests in joy and hope. Because He lives I can face tomorrow. Hallelujah!

3   The angel's face was like brilliant lightning. Heaven is the place of light and glory. He brought that light on his face, as Moses reflected the light of God's presence on his face, Exodus 34.29-35. The angel's clothing was white like snow. This speaks of the holiness of God satisfied by Christ's death, and the glory and majesty of God upheld. All this has been declared by the resurrection of the King.

4   The soldier-guards were totally overpowered. Fear shook them so violently they became paralyzed. Their brave "toughness" melted like wax. And no wonder! The might of one angel is greater than many thousands of men, see 2 Kings 19.35.

5   But what a contrast is here. To the faithful women the angel said, Don't **you** be afraid. In verse 4 is total fear; in verse 5 is **no** fear.

What makes the difference? Faith! Believers in Christ need not fear the holiness, power and majesty of God. Christ is risen, their Savior lives. Look at Romans 4.24,25; 2 Timothy 1.7.

6   1. *The Great Announcement:* He is not here! No, His disciples had not come and stolen the body. His enemies would have prevented that. But He is not here.

2. *The Great Explanation:* He has risen from the dead. On the cross He was the Victim. Now at the empty tomb He was the Victor.

3. *The Great Confirmation:* Just as He said. He **always** does what He says. He is the Faithful Witness, the Truth, and true to His word.

4. *The Great Invitation* — Come and see. The stone has been taken away, not to let Jesus out (He had already left).but to let believers in to see for themselves that the tomb is empty. We go out singing, My sins are gone, Praise the Lord.

7   But Come and See is closely followed by:

5. *The Great Command* — Go and Tell. Publish the Good News, share the blessing, go urgently and without delay.

6. *A Great Encouragement* — He goes before you, see John 10.4. Follow Him and enjoy His provision, protection and prosperity. This verse can also apply to His ascension into heaven to prepare a place there for us, as in John 14.1-3.

8   7. *A Great Joy* — this was the force which made them run in swift obedience to tell the disciples.

9   They suddenly were given even greater joy—Jesus Himself met them. He greeted them with the very common, "Greetings," like we say "good morning." The thrilled women threw themselves at His feet and worshiped Him.

10   His next word to them was, Don't be afraid. Perfect love casts out fear, 1 John 4.18. Again they are told, Go and tell. Whom? My brothers. What grace, the King calls His poor, failing, doubting disciples "My brothers." In grace He is not ashamed of them, Hebrews 2.10-15. Then He repeats the angel's instructions for them to go to Galilee. He would meet them there.

The Guard's Report, 28.11-15

11   Meanwhile the soldier-guards recovered (perhaps after the angels had left?) Did they creep away in shame and disgrace? At least they knew it was their duty to report the whole matter to the chief priests.

12   Their report must have stunned the chief priests. They called the Council together for a (secret) meeting to discuss what must be

done. They had to make some plans quickly. (They were well-practised at plotting and planning, as we have seen in chapter 26.3,4; 27.1,2,62-64; John 11.47 and 12.10,11.) It would never do to have the truth told to the public. When you reject truth all that's left is a lie. And they had good practice in lying also, John 8.44,45. Another plentiful thing they had was money. So they decided on this plan: Money plus lies plus more money and lies equals success.

1. First bribe the soldiers with a large sum of money. (The priests did not care to remember what the Law of Moses said about bribery, as in Exodus 23.8; Deuteronomy 16.18,19.)

2. Second, teach them to lie. With hands and pockets full of money, their ears are easily filled with lies: (1) His disciples came during the night, (2) they stole the body, (3) while we were sleeping. (Roman soldiers asleep on duty? that meant death for them!)

14   3. Next they promised to cover up for them if the Governor heard and started an investigation. They knew "large money" can persuade governors, too. (Compare Felix in Acts 24.26.)

15   So the soldiers (1) took the money. (Judas had done so, also, but it didn't do him any good, 26.15); (2) and spread the false stories. Matthew wrote that the Jews were still spreading them many years later when he wrote this book. Even today Satan is spreading lies about our King's life, death and resurrection, John 8.44.

The Great Commission, 28.16-20

Surely God had a real purpose in giving to us, right at this point, the King's Commission to His followers to spread the Truth to all nations. Satan's servants did as they were taught, v.15. Now the King's servants must do the same. But notice the contrast, as pointed out by an old missionary in Africa:

Satan: the Liar	Christ: the Truth
1. Claims obedience The soldiers did as they were taught	1. Claims obedience If you love Me, obey. John 14.15 1 John 5.3
2. We will stand behind you if you are in trouble. But contrast Judas, 27.4,5.	2. I am with you always. Hebrews 13.5,6. He never lets us down.
3. Bait—large money because of the large lie	3. No money mentioned. He gives much more—Himself.
4. Lie—say they stole Him	4. Truth—I am with you. I will **live** down the Jewish lie.

5. Followers go out spreading lies   5. Followers went out preaching the Truth everywhere, the Lord working with them, Mark 16.20.

Which master are you following and obeying?

16 In Galilee the disciples met their King on a mountain, where He had told them to go.

Jesus loved the mountains. Look up these references and write down what important things He did or said at each one:

Mark 3.13	_____	Matthew 18.12	_____
Matthew 4.8	_____	Matthew 21.1	_____
Matthew 5.1	_____	Matthew 24.3	_____
Matthew 14.23	_____	Matthew 26.30	_____
Matthew 15.29	_____	Matthew 28.16	_____
Matthew 17.1-13	_____	Acts 1.12	_____
Matthew 17.20 (& 21.21)	_____		

17 When they saw Him they worshiped Him. By faith this is always true for the believer. When the heart sees Him we worship Him.

But some doubted. Not some of the 11 since they had all seen Him before this. Probably the 500 of 1 Corinthians 15.6 were there and some of them were still doubting like Thomas did at first, John 20.24-28.

18 But the King clears away all doubts. In these last three verses the KING takes complete command as He claims total submission and obedience from His followers. He states that all authority in heaven and earth is His! He is Supreme—Lord of lords, King of kings, Lord of all. Revelation 19.16; Philippians 2.9-11.

19-20 **Therefore** His followers are to GO (remember this is the third time in this short chapter). They are to go forth, by His authority, under His control, doing His will. Going, they are to:

(1) Make disciples of **all** nations. A disciple is a learner who intends to follow. Discipling is more than merely bringing people to accept Christ as Savior; it includes making them followers and servants of the LORD.

(2) Baptize them. In their common language baptizing was dipping, immersing something in a liquid, like a cloth dipped into liquid dye to color it. All disciples are expected to be baptized in the Name of the Triune God. It is a testimony to the world that we belong to the King.

(3) Teach them all the King's commands. That is why this book of Matthew and all the other books of the New Testament were written —to teach us to obey **all** of our King's royal Law of Love.

And this Good News by Matthew ends with a precious promise by our wonderful King:

Surely	— the Royal Assurance - no doubts
I	— the Royal Person - the King Himself
will	— the Royal Promise - unfailing
be with you	— the Royal Presence
Always	— without interruption
to the very end	— without leaving you
of the age	— without end.

Matthew begins with Emmanuel, God with us, 1.23, and ends with I am, I will be with you, 28.20.

What more can His disciples need or want?

AMEN

Appendix 1

The Twelve Disciples

Why are the various lists of the twelve disciples not all the same? The comparative chart will help to identify them. The order given in Matthew is changed in other lists, as the numbers will show. Some suggest that Matthew listed the disciples by families, as brothers, for example, Peter and Andrew, sons of Jonas (John); James and John, sons of Zebedee. Possibly Philip and Bartholomew were brothers. Bartholomew of Matthew, Mark and Luke is called Nathanael in John. Both are next to Philip in all four gospels. Compare John 1.45 and 21.2. Philip led Nathanael to Jesus. It is possible that Thomas, the Twin, was brother to Matthew, and even James the Less, son of Alphaeus. But we cannot be sure. Lebbeus (in some old Bibles) and Thaddeus are not family names but seem to be names of affection in Matthew and Mark.

In Luke and Acts Judas, son of James, must be Thaddeus of Matthew and Mark. Simon the Zealot had been a member of the radical political party called Zealots. This name is used to distinguish him from Simon Peter. Judas Iscariot is always listed last. Iscariot means, Man of Kerioth, a town of Judea, cf. Joshua 15.25.

Mark lists them in order of importance, before the Cross. Peter, James and John lead, compare lists in Matthew 17.1 and 26.37.

Luke seems to follow Matthew's list by families. But he drops the affectionate name of Thaddeus and uses his proper name, Judas son of James.

John does not list the twelve disciples as a group. But we have shown which ones he does name and in which chapter.

Acts was written by Luke. Here he appears to list them in order of importance **after** the Cross, as: Peter, chap. 1-4; John, chap. 4 and 8; James, chap. 12.

The Twelve Disciples

MATTHEW 10 Matt. #	MARK 3 Matt. #		LUKE 6 Matt. #		JOHN Chap. Matt. #		ACTS 1 Matt. #	
1 Simon (Peter) son of John (Jonas)	Simon Peter	1	Simon Peter	1	(1) Andrew	2	Peter	1
2 Andrew son of John	James (son of Boanerges)	3	Andrew	2	(1) Simon Peter	1	John	4
3 James, son of Zebedee	John, son of Boanerges	4	James	3	(1) Philip	5	James	3
4 John, son of Zebedee	Andrew	2	John	4	(1) Nathanael (Bartholomew)	6	Andrew	2
5 Philip	Philip	5	Philip	5	(6) Judas Iscariot	12	Philip	5
6 Bartholomew	Bartholomew	6	Bartholomew	6	(11) Thomas (the Twin)	7	Thomas	7
7 Thomas (the twin)	Matthew (son of Alphaeus ?)	8	Matthew	8	(1) (John) called Disciple Jesus loved	4	Bartholomew	6
8 Matthew (tax collector)	Thomas (twin)	7	Thomas (twin)		(21) James son/Zebedee	3	Matthew	8
9 James (the Less) son of Alphaeus	James (son of Alphaeus	9	James (son of Alphaeus	9	(14) Judas son of James	10	James (son of Alphaeus)	9
10 Thaddeus (Lebbeus)	Thaddeus	10	Simon (Zealot)	11			Simon (Zealot)	11
11 Simon (Zealot) (Canaanite)	Simon (Zealot)	11	Judas son of James	10			Judas son of James	10
12 Judas Iscariot	Judas Iscariot	12	Judas Iscariot	12				

MATTHEW 13

Appendix 2

Parable	PERSONS			Seed	SOIL			HARVEST				Enemy
	Man	Servant	Woman		Field	Good	Bad	Barn	Fire	Birds	Thorns	
1. Sower	x			good	var.	x				x	x	
2. Darnel/weed	x	x		good & bad	x	x	x	x	x			x
3. Mustard seed	x			x	x		x			x		
4. Yeast			x									x
5. Hidden treasure	x				x							
6. Pearl	x											
7. Net		x				x	x					
8. Householder	x											
Meanings	Son of Man	The Angels		cf. Enemy: agent of evil	Good: sons of Kingdom. Also Word of God / Bad: sons of evil one	Field: the world / Soil — varying	True faith	Mere profession/pretending faith	Safety, salvation	Harvest: end of age / Fire: judgment	The evil one and his agents	Worldly cares	The evil one—Satan

Weeds	Tree	Meal	Yeast	Treasure	Cost	Net	House	Scope	PROGRESS OF CHRISTENDOM
								Given to the multitudes — Outward aspect—seen by all.	Good News to all. Truth. Some Fruit *
x									Counterfeit. False * added by enemy. Cults
	x								Growth of evil power Wicked agents inside. e.g. Modernism
		x	x						Evil developing puffs up
				x	x			Given to Disciples only — Inward aspect—seen by God.	Treasure valuable to King. Purchases world. Cost: death
				x	x				Treasure identified Pearl = church Greatest price
						x			End of age vs. 30,41,42 Eternal separation End of "Christendom"
				x			x		Summary: responsibility of instructed disciples Share treasure of Word.
Sons of the Evil One	Pride in power	Meal offering: fellowship	Evil growing	Hidden treasure in field: Israel set aside / Pearl: church in present age	Great price paid: precious blood of Christ				Interpreted by the King. *

Printed in Hong Kong